MAPPING THE
MEMORY

MAPPING THE
MEMORY

Understanding Your Brain to Improve Your Memory

RITA CARTER

Ulysses Press

Published in the U.S. by Ulysses Press
P.O. Box 3440
Berkeley, CA 94703
www.ulyssespress.com

First published as *Use your Brain to Beat Memory Loss* in Great Britain in 2005 by Cassell Illustrated, a division of Octopus Publishing Group Ltd.

Printed in Canada by Webcom Limited

10 9 8 7 6 5 4 3 2 1

ISBN-10: 1-56975-555-8
ISBN-13: 978-1-56975-555-6
Library of Congress Control Number: 2006903818

Editor: Joanne Wilson
Interior Design: DW Design
Cover Design: what!design@whatweb.com
Index: Indexing Specialists (UK) Ltd.
U.S. Editorial/Production: Matt Orendorff, Kathryn Brooks, Lily Chou

Distributed by Publishers Group West

Contents

Introduction

Have you ever thought that you would like a *really accurate memory*? One that can store *everything,* and recall it *clearly* whenever you want? Let me assure you, you do not want "perfect" memory. Human memory, like every other brain function, evolved to keep the person who has it alive, and what you need for that is, in some ways, the very opposite of what we think of as a "good" memory. Normal memory is selective, vague, unreliable, prejudicial and ultimately forgetful. If it wasn't, we would be in trouble.

The purpose of human memory is to use past events to guide future actions, and keeping a perfect and complete record of the past is not necessarily the best way to achieve this. The ability to *generalize* from experience is important too. When you first start to drive a car, for example, you learn from the moment you get into the first vehicle what each pedal does. Subsequently, whenever you drive a new vehicle, you assume that the position of the pedals is the same. The specific memory of the layout of one particular car merged with other specifics to form a piece of general knowledge.

Memory problems

Although a perfect memory is neither desirable nor necessary, to function well in day-to-day life you need to store a vast and fairly accurate database of words, names, facts, dates, plans and locations. You need to be able to hold plans of action in your mind just long enough for you to carry them out. If you find yourself regularly failing in this, and if it is disrupting your life, then you could use help.

When people talk about having a bad memory, they usually mean that they forget things. But there are many other types of memory problems, for example memories that come to mind clearly but don't seem to match with facts we know to be true. There are also memories that blur into one another and recollections that get transposed or muddled.

It is possible, too, to remember things too well. Most of us know what it is like to wake up in the night and be assaulted by a flashback of an embarrassing social encounter. More seriously, many people are haunted by memories of traumatic incidents. Pain itself can recur as a memory – if a part of your body hurts enough, for long enough, your brain lays down the experience as a memory and may replay it long after the injury has healed.

Causes and cures

There are dozens of causes of memory failure. Some are temporary – little glitches that mean nothing. Others are due to illnesses, such as fevers, or the effect of alcohol or medicinal or recreational drugs. Still others are due to damage or degeneration. The problem is often reversible, either by treating the underlying cause or by learning to use your brain in a different way. Unlike other organs the brain is amazingly pliable – if it is damaged it can often rewire itself. It is also capable – up to a point – of producing new cells.

Helping yourself

This book shows you how you can *help yourself* to have a better memory. It tells the fascinating story of how your brain makes memories, explores the mechanics of learning and recall, and explains why specific memory failings occur. From this you will discover how certain habits of thought and ways of experiencing the world can make your memory function more efficiently. There is also a comprehensive directory of prescribed drugs, natural remedies and lifestyle changes that may improve your memory. Finally, there are some practical "tricks" to help you to recall things better.

This book does not, however, promise to give you a "perfect" memory. Fortunately, nobody has that.

Common causes of memory failure

- "Normal" age-related brain changes
- Dementia
- Brain injuries from an accident or stroke
- Diseases affecting the brain
- Prescription or recreational drugs
- Sleep disorders
- Depression
- Stress

Part One
Making memories

1. Understanding what memory is

"The charm, one might say the genius of memory, is that it is choosy, chancy and temperamental: it rejects the edifying cathedral and indelibly photographs the small boy outside, chewing a hunk of melon in the dust."

Elizabeth Bowen, New York, September 1955

What is memory?

The conventional way of talking about human memory is to liken it to a database – a library storing facts, for example; or a video or DVD holding a cinematic representation of past experiences.

These analogies are commonsensical, but inaccurate. It is more helpful to think of memory as a process rather than as a static repository of information. The storage element of memory is only one aspect of a highly dynamic system that is closely intertwined with thought, emotion, perception and action. Indeed, you could regard almost all cognitive function as memory of sorts.

Consciousness itself might even depend on memory, because you have to hold something in your mind – an image or a thought – for at least a fraction of a second before you become aware of it. The dynamic process of memory is key to its functioning, and the better that memory – and all its constituent parts – functions, the better our memory serves us on a day-to-day level.

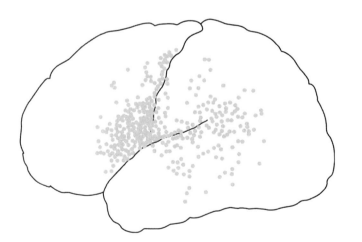

Canadian brain surgeon Wilder Penfield identified the brain regions that produced memories by probing the cortex during operations on conscious epileptic patients. The dots show places where stimulation elicited snatches of memory during his investigations.

The memory process

The memory process can be broken down into several distinct stages, and a glitch in any one of these stages can give rise to problems.

Stage 1: selection

Only a tiny amount of what we encounter is committed to memory – a smattering of events, a fraction of the facts we come across, a few habitual movement sequences. The vast majority of our experiences are not selected by our brain and pass us by as though they never occurred.

Stage 2: lay-down

The experiences that are selected for memorizing may stay encoded (stored) for just a split second or for a lifetime. The ones that stay go through an elaborate process of consolidation that can take up to two years.

Stage 3: recollection

Even if memories are selected and then stored firmly, they may remain inaccessible if the next stage – recollection – is faulty. But recollection is not a simple matter of re-activating stored information. It also involves *changing* memories to incorporate new information. Sometimes this part of the process causes memories to be changed in a damaging way, but if it did not occur we would lose much of the fluidity of thought that allows us to act intelligently. Forgetting is not, in itself, a bad thing. It is, as we shall see, essential.

Forgetting: what can go wrong?

Stage	What is meant to happen	What can go wrong	Typical effects
Selection	The brain is designed to store information that it thinks will be useful at a later date, allowing the rest to pass by unnoted.	Important events are neglected or unimportant ones are selected.	You fail to recall a person's name, but clearly remember the mole on their nose.
Lay-down	Experience that is selected for memorizing is stored in such a way that it is associated with relevant pre-existing memories and retained for an appropriate period.	Information may be "mis-filed" (1), or the process of lay-down may fail (2).	(1) You separately lay down both the name and the face, but you don't connect them. (2) New events and facts do not "go in," so learning is difficult and old memories seem more vivid than recent ones.
Recollection	Current events (including the conscious desire to check back on something) should stimulate the recollection of appropriate memories, perhaps those that can guide future actions.	Current events do not "pull up" useful memories.	Inability to remember words, names, routes, people or events. You know the information is there but you can't grasp it.
Change	Each time a memory is recalled it is altered slightly to accommodate new information.	Alteration may create false memories.	The new memory is significantly different from the original event.
Forgetting	Events start to be forgotten as soon as they have been registered unless they are constantly refreshed. This is essential – a brain full of unused memories would be literally "clogged up" with unnecessary information.	Important or useful information is forgotten (1), or inessential or damaging memories are not (2).	(1) General forgetfulness, without even the realization that you have forgotten something. (2) Unwanted memories swamp your thoughts, such as a phrase from a pop song that keeps going around in your head or being haunted by a casually glimpsed image of suffering.

Remembering to remember

 It was when I found myself standing in the kitchen with a hammer in one hand and the cat in the other – and no idea at all why I was there – that I really started to worry. I had been doing this sort of thing all my life, as well as more usual things like losing my car keys and forgetting birthdays, but I was convinced it was getting worse. I started monitoring myself for signs of dementia, but I found that the very act of thinking about what I was doing reduced the number of times I forgot things. So, without intending to, I trained myself to live more "in the moment," thinking about what I was doing now rather than daydreaming about what I might be doing tomorrow. It has made me more efficient generally, as well as improving my memory. But I still drift off into dreamland sometimes and get yanked back to earth by the smell of burning toast…. It's the price you pay, I think, for having imagination.

The hammer was for crushing the cat's worming pill, incidentally. It came back to me later, but by that time the cat had taken refuge under the bed. I don't think she ever did get dosed, but it didn't seem to matter.

Claire, 42, novelist

2. How memories are constructed

"A memory is what is left when something happens and does not completely unhappen."

Edward de Bono

Raw materials

The word "memory" is usually taken to mean recall, but, as we have seen, it is far more than that. Before you can recall something you have to have some trace of it in your brain. By trace, I mean that the brain must be primed to reproduce the cognitive state of the original experience (see "Long-term potentiation," page 27).

To have a trace of something you need to have learned it – to have gone through the "lay-down" part of the process. And in order to lay something down you have to have experienced it. The experience doesn't have to be conscious, as we shall see, but it must be strong enough to be registered and to have caused a change in the brain.

Memory begins, then, with perception. Every waking moment (and a lot of the time when we are asleep) the brain is taking in information from outside, via the senses, and from inside itself. Let's leave the "inside" bit for a moment and consider just what comes in from our environment.

The world we experience does not really exist. At least, not in the way it seems. "Grass," "sunshine," "melodies" and "scent" are not intrinsically green or warm, tuneful or pleasant – our brain makes them this way. All there is outside is energy: molecules made up of atoms in greater or lesser states of excitation, lightwaves and soundwaves. Our sense organs have evolved to respond to some of these things. A particular range of light and soundwaves, for example, trigger a response in our eyes and ears, while atoms in a certain state of arousal – what we call "hot" – have an effect on our peripheral, or outer, nerves. When these responses occur, electrical messages are sent via nerve cells to the specialized nerve cells in the brain, called neurons. The brain then "constructs" the signals into the objects that we think of as the furniture of the universe – the sights, sounds and smells we encounter in our environment.

The construction process

One way to think of this construction process is to imagine the brain as a factory that uses the signals from our senses as raw material for experience. The factory comprises a number of parallel assembly lines that converge to produce a single moment of experience. Let's look at one such assembly line – the one that deals with visual information – and see how it turns the signals from the eye into an image.

The back part of the brain – roughly from the crown of your head to the nape of your neck – is responsible for processing sensory information (apart from smell, which takes a different, more primitive route). The "higher" cognitive functions – thinking, planning, introspecting – are towards the front of the brain. Right at the very back of the brain lies the start of the visual processing assembly line, an area called V1.

When lightwaves hit the eyeball, they stimulate nerve cells along a path that eventually leads to V1 in the visual cortex, where certain cells respond by firing electrical signals. If V1 is excited enough by this signal from the eye, it jogs the next part of the brain into action and those cells then fire up their neighbors, and so on. Each set of cells, when activated, adds a specific element to the image that is being made. One group adds color, another shape, a third registers movement, and so on. The image therefore moves forward, as though on a conveyor belt, accumulating more and more elements, until eventually it has all the components – shape, color, location, movement, size and so on – that we expect of a visual perception.

However, it still has a long way to go before it *is* a visual perception. At this stage – a third of a second or so after the lightwaves hit the eye – the information is still unconscious. In order to become a conscious experience it has to be bound with information that is being processed along other assembly lines – the one that is constructing the sound coming in at that time, the one that is generating emotion, the one that is making the

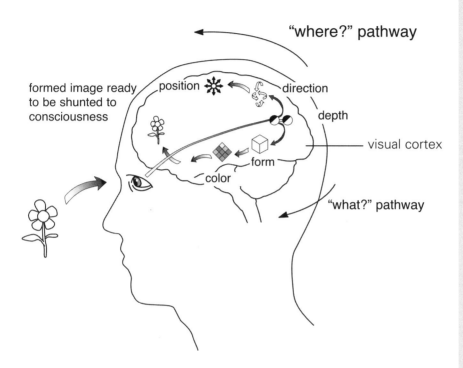

"where?" pathway

formed image ready to be shunted to consciousness

position

direction

depth

visual cortex

form

color

"what?" pathway

The brain factory
Each part of the brain specializes in a particular task. In the sensory areas, for example, there are specific modules that are concerned with color, shape and form. Raw visual material – in this case the sight of a flower – is sent along assembly lines that work out what the thing is and where it is and so on. Information is also sent to parts of the brain that respond to it emotionally, and others that prepare the body to act on it. Most incoming signals do not excite the brain enough to prompt it to form a conscious experience. Those that do, however, have the potential to become memories.

bodily sensation of the moment, and so on. Once that has been done the resulting sensory "package" still has to be recognized. That is, the brain has to make sense of the image – to understand that it is a cat, say, and not a cup. Only after all this has been completed do we experience a flash of conscious experience.

The majority of images never make it to the end of the assembly line because the brain is just not excited enough by most incoming information to bother to construct it. Any incoming information that is constructed, however, is now in a form that might – or might not – come to be a memory.

Short-term and long-term memory

Experiences, as we have seen, are the raw materials from which memories are made. But how does a fleeting pattern of neuronal activity – a single moment of experience – get to be laid down in the brain in such a way that it can be repeated? And why do some experiences linger for just a few seconds or minutes, while others stay for a lifetime?

Memory can be divided up into two broad categories: short-term and long-term. Within these two categories there are also several sub-types (see "Systems within systems," pages 38–39).

Short-term memories generally stay with us for just as long as we need them. Telephone numbers that are only needed once are a classic example of the stuff of short-term memory. If you look up a number and then go to the phone and punch it in, once the person answers you have no further pressing need for the number so you will start to forget it. By the end of the conversation you will probably have no (conscious) idea of what the number was. Of course, some telephone numbers (your own, for example) *become* long-term memories, but the vast majority of numbers that we use in a lifetime are dumped from memory very quickly.

Words, in contrast to telephone numbers, tend to become long-term memories more readily. If you look up a word in a dictionary, and that word is important to your understanding of something significant, the chances are that its definition will become a piece of knowledge that stays with you for life. This is particularly likely if you come across the word again soon after (which, oddly, often seems to happen with new words). Hence we build up a large vocabulary that is more or less permanently "on tap." We may not always be able to access the words on cue, but they are encoded (stored) in a hard-to-lose way that the once-used telephone number is not.

So what happens in the brain to sort the telephone numbers from the words? Basically, it is due to a difference in the way the numbers and words are processed. Short-term memories are dealt with by what is known as "working memory" (see pages 46, 48), a system that keeps currently useful information "hot" until its purpose is fulfilled. Longer-lasting memories are initially held in working memory too – but they then get transformed into more stable entities by a further process called long-term potentiation (see page 27).

Those memories that become part of the permanent conscious identity of a person – their clutch of vivid childhood memories, their biographical details and so on – go through yet a further construction process (see pages 52–54) that can take up to two years to complete.

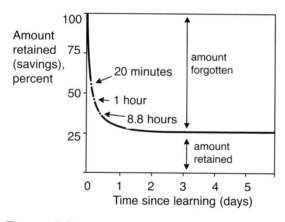

Repetition

Repetition is the key to memory. A short-term memory, as its name suggests, remains only for as long as it is repeated. In the case of a telephone number, for example, the sound of it and the sight of it is replayed by working memory until we no longer need it. If you continued to repeat the number after you needed it, it would eventually become a long-term memory. This is the basis of learning by rote.

The forgetting curve
Information is lost to the memory very quickly unless you work hard to retain it. Even carefully memorized information is unlikely to make it into long-term memory unless it has some kind of emotional significance. The "forgetting curve" (left), devised by German psychologist Hermann Ebbinghaus, shows the rapidity with which non-significant material (in this case "nonsense" syllables) is "lost." Ebbinghaus found that most forgetting takes place very soon after learning. If it "sticks" for three days or more, it is set for a long future. Meaningful information has a far less steep "forgetting curve."

Mental arithmetic

 I run a little farm store, and on weekends I sometimes corral the kids in to help serve. I am hopeless at anything to do with numbers, whereas both my children are near the top of their classes in math. So I was shocked, at first, to find that they needed to use a calculator for the simplest transaction, whereas I could do most of the adding-up in my head. When we talked about it, I found it was because I was drawing on my memory of multiplication tables. They were drummed into us so often at school that I can still do them – up to the twelve times table – without thinking. The children have never learned them because every time they need to know what six eights are they punch a few buttons and the answer comes up. They don't need to transfer it from short-term memory to long-term memory, I guess, because they assume there will always be a calculator on hand to do the work for them.

Marilyn, 60, farmer

Memorability

The difference the order of things makes to their memorability is large. Experiments show that the final items in a list are more than twice as likely to be remembered than mid-list items. This might be one reason why people whose last names start with a letter near the top of the alphabet are, on average, more successful than those with names in the middle range. The effect of always being called first (for school attendance and so on) may have made them stand out as more memorable figures, and thus endowed them with the benefit of more attention from people who could help them. It might also be the reason why most people are so determined to have the "last word" in an argument – the chances are that a parting remark will have more effect than anything said in the middle of a conversation.

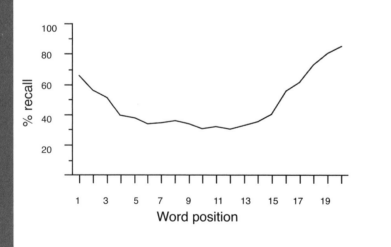

The primacy and recency effects
If you hear a list of random nouns – 20 or so words like "apple," "scissors" or "butterfly," and then try to recall what they were you will probably find it easier to repeat the first couple of words (a phenomenon called the "primacy effect") and the last couple (the "recency effect"). It is thought that memory is better for the words read last because they are still being "echoed" in working memory. The primacy effect may be because those words have had a little time to start becoming long-term memories. It is also more likely that you pay greater attention to the first words on the list because you have not, at that point, been distracted by other words.

Laying down the past

Consciousness is not, as it seems, a continuous stream. Rather it is made up of a series of "frames" – each one following on so fast from the previous one that they seem to merge seamlessly, like the individual stills that create a moving film. If we are very excited, these "blips" of experience run at the rate of hundreds of frames per second; or the rate can dip to just a couple of frames if we are unstimulated.

Each frame of consciousness is created by a particular pattern of neuronal firing. That is, some of the billions of cells in our brains are firing together in synchrony. It is a little like an illuminated advertising sign made up of thousands of different light bulbs, flashing on and off in different combinations to display dozens of different images. A moment of consciousness is like one particular light-bulb image.

Consciousness is the sum of thoughts, feelings, perceptions and emotions that a person can report on at any one moment. The "reporting" part is important, because it is quite plausible that we are fleetingly aware of much more than we can describe, even to ourselves. These are the impressions that can be made into conscious memories.

Although we know quite a lot about what consciousness is like, no one knows what it is. As far as we know the universe is entirely physical, yet mental constructs do not seem to be material at all. This intuition has created the notion – expressed most famously by the French philosopher Descartes – that consciousness is part of an immaterial, "spiritual" realm. This commonsense idea conflicts, however, with current scientific knowledge that suggests that even if there is a non-material realm of some sort, it could not possibly have any effect on the physical world. Conscious decisions, for example, could not cause the body to move.

When neurons fire together they are altered slightly so that they have a tendency to fire together again. A single synchronous firing produces only a weak tendency, and if those particular neurons are not stimulated to fire together again fairly quickly (by a similar stimulus to the first) the cells will go back to how they were. If, however, the original stimulus is repeated, the cells undergo a permanent change, so the links between the neurons are strengthened. It is these neuronal links that create a memory, and they are there even when the memory is not actually being recalled.

■ To *have a memory* of something means that your brain has undergone changes that make it likely to reproduce the neuronal firing pattern corresponding to a previous experience, or a fact that you have come across before.

■ To *remember the event* is the actual pattern re-firing. Short-term memories are created by a "weak" linkage that occurs after just a few simultaneous neuronal firings. They will last only for as long as the cells that produced the experience still have a tendency to spark up together. Long-term memories, however, are created by a further process that involves creating new links between cells (see right).

Kandel's experiments with Aplysia

Eric Kandel of Columbia University was awarded the 2000 Nobel Prize for his work on the cellular basis of memory. Kandel showed that *short-term memory involves changes in already existing synapses*, whereas *long-term memory involves creating new synapses*.

Most of Kandel's work was done on the mollusk Aplysia, which is popular with researchers because it has relatively few, very large, neurons. This means that changes in the neurons associated with experience are much easier to detect and study in Aplysia than in more complicated animals.

Creating new synapses

The molecular changes that underlie memory have not been directly observed in the human brain, but researchers at the University of California, San Diego, have photographed them happening in living cells in the laboratory. The cells were removed from the brain and then subjected to stimuli that mimics the signals they would receive during a learning experience if they were still within the brain.

The researchers discovered that when they stimulated a neuron once, a molecule in it called actin temporarily moved towards neighboring neurons. Actin is present in many cells throughout the body, and is associated with growth and cellular restructuring. The activity in the first cell also stimulated the movement of actin in neighboring neurons. Those changes were temporary, however, lasting for about three to five minutes and disappearing within five to ten minutes. If the neuron was stimulated four or more times within an hour, however, they found that cells created new "docking points" – synapses – with their neighbors, creating what is probably an irreversible alteration in the cells' wiring.

Long-term potentiation (LTP)

Memories are encoded when groups of neurons are linked together and fire together in a pattern they have formed previously. The links between individual cells are formed by a process called long-term potentiation.

A) Cell 1 receives a stimulus that makes it fire. This activity acts as a stimulus to Cell 2, which also fires. The second cell is chemically changed by this – receptors that are normally hidden inside the cell membrane are brought to the surface. These make Cell 2 more responsive to stimuli from Cell 1, and it will stay in this "alert" state for hours or perhaps even days.

B) If Cell 1 fires again while Cell 2 is alert, it need do so only weakly to set off Cell 2. Each time the two cells fire together their mutual sensitivity, or "link," is reinforced. Eventually they are "bound" together so firmly that they may fire together for the rest of their lifetime in the brain.

C) When two cells fire together their combined activity is likely to be enough to trigger a neighboring cell to which they are both attached, even if their links to it are relatively weak. If this happens repeatedly the neighboring cell gets bound with the first two. Memories are formed by the firing of networks of neighboring cells that are linked in this way.

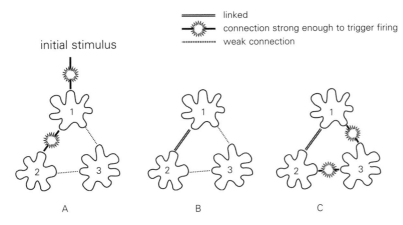

initial stimulus

═════ linked
⚡ connection strong enough to trigger firing
··········· weak connection

A   B   C

The hippocampus

If you lifted up the gray, wrinkled surface of the brain and looked beneath it, you would find a cluster of strange-shaped organs nestling in the center. One of these is the hippocampus. This complex mechanism plays an essential part in turning short-term memories into long-term ones. It is also essential for recalling those memories. Whenever you think of an event in your past, the hippocampus springs into action and retrieves it.

As we shall see, memories are not stored in little clumps, but are distributed around the brain like nodes on a spider's web (see pages 32–35). However, all memories – all the ones that you can actually describe, that is – are linked to the hippocampus rather like satellites around a mother ship.

As we have seen, all conscious experience exists, for a few seconds at least, as a memory (see page 12) – something that happens, and goes on happening in the mind for as long as we repeat it. Some of this is handled almost entirely by working memory (see pages 46, 48), but anything that is particularly striking – and thus may be needed for future reference – is extracted from the maelstrom of momentary experience and sent off for processing.

The hippocampus works in a manner similar to a one-way road system in a city center. The traffic that enters it is those items in experience that we may want to lay down. This information comes in from working memory and loops around coiled layers of tissue. On the way most of it quietly fades away – that is, the neuronal activity that represents it simply fizzles out. The strongest of it, though, goes right around the loop and is then played back to the parts of the brain that first registered it. A striking visual stimulus, for example, comes in via the visual cortex, is held for a while in working memory, then travels to the hippocampus, goes around the one-way system, and is then sent back to the visual cortex, where it is replayed as a distant echo of the original sight. Most of this incoming traffic does not have the "energy" to make it back to its source. It fades away on its travels and is lost to recall forever. However, particularly strong stimuli – those that really get the neurons excited – make the trip repeatedly. If a

The hippocampus is a curious formation that lies in the center of the brain. It records conscious experiences and then "files" some of them in other parts of the brain. Damage to the hippocampus results in profound memory disorders.

stimulus passes through the hippocampus often enough it creates permanent changes that are reinforced by subsequent visits. The experience has made the first step towards becoming a permanent fixture.

Encoding something in the hippocampus is not the end of the story, though. Over a longer period – probably about two years – the hippocampus continues to process its store of memories. Effectively it splits them into component parts – sights, sounds, thoughts and emotions – and replays them to the parts of the brain where they originated. Sensory impressions, for example, will be replayed to the appropriate cells in the sensory cortices – the "gray matter" that forms the wrinkled surface of the brain. These replays then bring about permanent changes in these cortical cells too. In other words, it duplicates the memories in their component parts, distributing them around the brain.

Thereafter the hippocampus is more like a central index than a memory storage. When a stimulus from working memory enters it that is similar in some way to a piece of information it has processed before, the hippocampus retrieves that previous experience by re-igniting the neural patterns that first gave rise to it. The hippocampus sparks off the recall of the whole experience.

The hippocampus during sleep

The hippocampus does a lot of its "lay-down" work while we sleep. During waking hours the onslaught of new information from the world outside keeps it busy selecting and processing current information. When we fall asleep, however, this bombardment ceases and the hippocampus starts to "trawl over" what it has recently dealt with. Recently laid neural patterns spontaneously replay. Some of them surface in dreams. So if you have spent the day chopping vegetables, the "chopping vegetables" pattern may therefore spring up during a phase of REM sleep (the stage in the sleep cycle during which the body has increased brain activity and dreams occur) and infiltrate whatever else happens to be occupying your mind. Chopped carrots may therefore be juxtaposed in a dream with images of fish, feelings of fear and the sound of bells.

The hippocampus continues to work on consolidating experience into memory, even when we are in "quiet sleep" – the stages when we seem to be unconscious of anything. In this state, it links new experience to old, filling in the web.

Finding a memory replacement

Scientists are working to make a replacement hippocampus that could take over some of the cognitive tasks lost to people with dementia or brain injury. Researchers at the University of Southern California in Los Angeles have devised a mathematical model of how the hippocampus works and have created a silicon chip that mimics the organ. Now they are working on ways to "slot" the chip into the brain so that the natural biological tissue interfaces seamlessly with the artificial prosthesis.

The team produced their model by taking slices of rat hippocampus and stimulating them repeatedly to discover which electrical input produced a corresponding output. Putting the information gained from various slices together gave the team a mathematical model of the entire hippocampus.

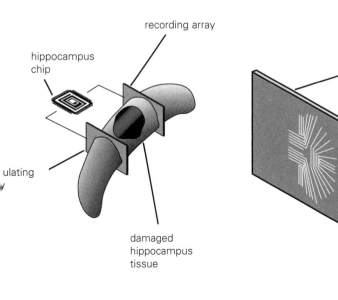

recording array

hippocampus chip

multiple electrodes like these are placed on each array

ulating

damaged hippocampus tissue

This diagram shows how a memory "chip" might work to carry out the job of a damaged hippo-campus. Electrodes (shown, right) make up memory chips that approximate the structure of nerve tissue within a slice of hippo-campus. One such array records and the other transmits the neuronal activity received to other parts of the brain.

Weaving the web

We have seen that the hippocampus lays down and accesses "declarative" memories – that is, episodes and facts that you can bring to mind consciously. However, these memories are not stored in one place, but throughout the brain – as potential firing patterns – in a way that resembles a huge cobweb. Each "element" of a memory – the sight, sound, word or emotion that it consists of – is encoded in the part of the brain that originally created it. Each one, then, is the same as a current perception, except that the information that created it comes from within the brain, instead of externally via the sense organs.

Take, for example, a memory of a brown dog that you once owned. The "brown" part of the memory is created by the "color" area of the visual cortex; the words "dog" and, say, "Rover," are in the language area, and so on. The hippocampus accesses the memory by triggering all these elements together. Parts of the memory, in turn, will be associated with other things: a brown cat; a wolf you saw one day at the zoo; the day that Rover got lost. So once the "Rover" memory is sparked up, it jogs these related memories into action too. And if it jogs them hard enough they come to mind. Hence one thing "reminds" us of another.

The incredible thing about our memory system is that it allows new events to be integrated into old ones, so that experience builds on experience. Every brown dog we see "maps" on to the memories of Rover, so we come to have a general familiarity with dogs rather than just a specific memory of Rover. If memories were not stored in this way, the world in our heads would consist of billions of splintered memories that had no relation to one another. So, for example, a child might have a memory of her mother in a yellow dress, and another of her mother in a pink dress. She may have a memory of her mother looking cross, and another of her mother laughing. If these various images were not connected, she would seem to have dozens of mothers ("yellow-dress mother," "pink-dress mother" and so on), but no *general* idea of her mother at all. Each time she saw her mother in a different outfit, she would need to learn afresh who her mother was.

The other huge benefit of this distributed storage system is that it makes long-term memories more or less indestructible. If they were held in a single brain area, damage to that specific place – from a stroke or head injury, for example – would eradicate the memory entirely. As it is, brain trauma and degeneration nibble away at memories but rarely destroy them altogether. You may lose a person's name, but not the memory of their face. Rover may, over time, lose his brownness – but the day he got lost will remain vividly in your memory.

Tapping into the web

Memories are like wolves at the door – they are continually looking for a way to pop up in consciousness. The ones that are most persistent are those closest to a person's current concerns. Incoming information – moment-by-moment experience – constantly jogs out relevant memories. If these cues are not conducive to thinking about a particular concern – if, for example, you are in a situation that "takes your mind off" a worry – these "hot" memories can be kept out of consciousness. But if you are in a situation where the environment is not providing you with sufficient meaningful diversions, the memories will pop up again, unbidden.

An experiment devised by Diana Deutsch, a professor of psychology at the University of California, San Diego, demonstrates how easily we revert to reminiscing on current concerns when we do not have enough interesting information coming in. She presented volunteers with the sound of fairly neutral words being repeated over and over again. After a while listeners began to "hear" words that weren't actually on the track. According to Deutsch, who has played her sound demonstrations to hundreds of her students, the extraneous words that people hear that aren't actually on the track are quite subjective, often reflecting the listener's current state of mind.

Deutsch likens the effect to the Rorschach inkblot test, in which people see meaningful images in what is actually just a randomly splashed blob of ink. Such perceptions tend to reflect things that people are concerned about, sometimes unconsciously. She says, "If someone is on a diet they tend to hear words related to food or dieting. Women often hear things of a romantic nature, whereas men do not. Even native speakers of languages other than English tend to hear words and phrases in their native language.

"Although this sounds quite strange and people have insisted that I must have inserted new words into the tracks, the explanation is rather simple. The phantom words are generated by the brain in an attempt to create order out of the chaos of sound that is presented. This also explains why listeners tend to hear words that are meaningful to them. "

In another experiment Deutsch played listeners two differently pitched "test" tones that are separated by a time interval during which other tones are heard. Under these conditions, most people find it difficult to tell whether the two test tones are the same or different in pitch, even though they can ignore the other tones. However, when spoken words were presented during this interval instead of other tones, most listeners had no trouble recalling the pitch of the earlier tones.

"This experiment," said Deutsch, "shows a striking dissociation between musical tones and spoken words in memory, and indicates that separate memory stores are responsible for retaining different aspects of sound. "

"It's surprising how much memory is built around things unnoticed at the time."

Barbara Kingsolver,
Animal Dreams

3. Types of memory

"How it came back to me! That peculiar feeling ... that we used to call 'Church'... that sweet corpsy smell, the rustle of Sunday dresses, the wheeze of the organ, the spot of light from the hole in the window creeping slowly up the nave ... For a moment I didn't merely remember it, I was *in* it."

George Orwell, *Coming Up for Air,* 1939

Systems within systems

Although all the different aspects of memory are very closely related and are interactive, it is possible to split memory into sub-systems, according to what each sub-system does and in which part of the brain. The main sub-systems are:

1. Episodic memory

Episodic memories, as their name suggests, are rather like re-runs of experience: they repeat – albeit usually quite faintly – the sensations (especially sights and sounds) and the emotions that attended an original episode or event. Crucially, these scenes always have the individual who is experiencing them at their center – they are *personal* memories, things that happened (or seemed to have happened) to the person who is remembering them, and they are *unique* to that individual. Most episodic memories unfold in time, like a movie, although they may also appear as single-frame "flashbacks."

2. Semantic memory

This is the term used for the laying down and retrieving of facts, for example that the Eiffel Tower is in Paris, that World War II took place between 1939 and 1945 or that acorns come from oak trees. They differ from episodic memories in that they *seem* to "stand alone," without any connection to personal experience. Thus your memory that the Eiffel Tower is in Paris is for all practical purposes identical to my memory that it is.

3. Working memory

This is the capacity to hold information in your mind for just long enough to work out what to do with it. The classic example is keeping a telephone number intact for long enough to dial the number. Most mental tasks depend on working memory – it sorts your thoughts, guides your actions and organizes cognitive processes so you can do several things at the same time.

4. Procedural memory

Procedural memories are those that allow you to carry out the countless actions that you do every day without having to think consciously about them. Walking, for example, relies on procedural memory, as do swimming and riding a bike. Unlike semantic and episodic memories, procedural memories are generally unconscious.

5. Implicit memory

This, too, is unconscious – you could think of implicit memories as ones we don't know we have. Although they do not occur as thoughts, implicit memories affect our actions in subtle ways. For example, if, for no discernable reason, you find yourself feeling uncomfortable with someone you have just met, it may be that you have an implicit memory of someone unpleasant who looked a little like them.

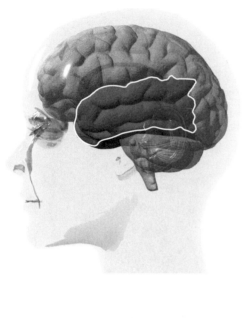

Over time memories are encoded in the outer (cortical) areas of the brain. Sounds and words, for example, are encoded in the temporal cortex (outlined).

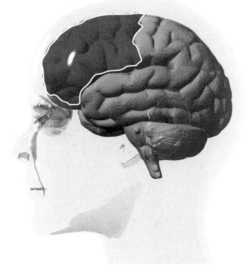

The frontal lobes (outlined) are concerned with working memory and pulling out and selecting long-term memories to guide current actions.

Times past – episodic memory

Episodic memories – events that actually happened to you – are not generally static snapshots, but a sequence of frames, so that the recollection (like the original experience) unfolds in time. However, few events hold our attention continuously for more than a second or two, so memories tend to be fragmented. Even if we seem to have a "complete" memory of something that took several hours to happen, closer analysis will normally reveal that what we really recall is a series of fragments. Two people witnessing the same event will usually lay down different fragments of it, and if they compare their recollection they will find that one of them can often "fill in" moments that are missing from the other's memory.

Only a tiny fraction of the millions of events that happen to us every day are stored as memories. And of those, only a tiny proportion persist beyond the point at which they are relevant to action. Think about something you did yesterday – catching a bus, say. You may recall seeing it appear around the corner, or stepping into it, or paying your fare. But can you really re-run the whole event – from the moment the bus appeared to the moment you got off it? You might *think* you can – but on close examination you will find that what you have retained of the bus ride is, if anything, very patchy indeed. Can you recall the other passengers, for example? The color of the seats? The traffic that passed by as you looked through the window? You probably noticed some of these things and memorized them for a few seconds, but you would have kept them in mind only for as long as it took for your brain to work out that they held no special significance and could safely be discarded. Most of the information coming in to your senses during the bus ride was probably lost before it even became conscious.

Episodic memories are therefore the actual slivers of experience that *do* get stored. Very few of them are laid down in sufficient detail to provide the sort of detailed replay described above, and most of them will simply be "highlights" rather than a continuous strand. Even the most vivid memories are usually composed of just a few moments of real time – that childhood picnic when you first met a donkey and were terrified by its flapping ears … can you remember what happened *after* you fled into your mother's arms? Or the journey home?

How episodic memory works

Recalling an episodic memory is not the purely mental act that it might appear to be because the crucial thing about this type of recall is that it reproduces – albeit in a degraded form – the physical state that the person was in when the event occurred. This includes the emotions and sensory experiences that occurred at that time. If you thought about a time when you were caught in a snowstorm without a coat, for example, your body would actually reproduce some of the processes that were brought on by the cold and you would actually *feel* a little cooler. To recall an episodic memory is therefore to re-live it.

The way episodic memory works is that every event you experience is a specific brain state – that is, a condition in which certain brain cells are firing and others are not. If you are caught in a snowstorm the neurons that will be triggered will include – among billions of others – the neurons that process the white of the snow, the ones that register the changes of temperature on your skin, the ones that prompt you to quicken your return home and so on. At the same time, you will probably have neurons firing that are the recognition that this will mean your train will be late; and others that are memories of *past* snowstorms; and maybe there will even be some neurons making you feel anxious – prompted by yet other neurons that are reminding you that you promised to be home early to put up a Christmas tree. Each of these unique, phenomenally complex brainstates is an experience, and if that same state – an identical pattern of neural firing – could be reproduced it would place the person in *precisely* the same condition as it did originally. You could be basking on a desert island, watching dolphins and sipping a piña colada, but if your nervous system were to flip into the state it was in during the snowstorm, you would be oblivious to everything around you. It would be a memory – but as far as you would know you would be right back there in the snowstorm.

In practice, of course, this does not happen. Episodic memories are only *loose* reproductions of previous brain states. It is vital that they are this way, because if they weren't we would hallucinate, rather than remember. Which, as we shall see, is one of the things that can happen when memory goes wrong (see page 69).

Interaction of the brain's hemispheres

The two hemispheres of the brain are connected by a thick band of tissue called the corpus callosum that allows information to be shared between them. Episodic memories tend to be suffused with emotion in a way that semantic memories are not. They therefore require more "input" from the right hemisphere of the brain, which tends to specialize in the emotional aspects of perception. The role of the right hemisphere in enhancing episodic memories was demonstrated by a study carried out with people who, for hereditary reasons, were believed to have unusually large numbers of connective fibers in the corpus callosum and therefore able to bring more "right hemisphere" information to bear on what they remembered.

The results of the study appeared to show that, because the brain's hemispheres work together to help us remember events, people whose hemispheres work together more actively (because they have more communication fibers) remember events better than they remember facts.

Remembering facts – semantic memory

Semantic memories are the facts that we distill and store from our stream of experience – together they comprise a personal built-in encyclopedia. They differ from episodic memories in that they do not generally evoke conscious emotions or sensations, and the person remembering them is not part of them. So, for example, you could have a semantic memory that Charlie Chaplin starred in the film *Modern Times*. You don't know how you know it, but somehow you have learned it and now you can state it as a fact. You could also have an episodic memory of a rainy Sunday afternoon when you watched *Modern Times* on television and learned that the funny man with a moustache was a famous comedian called Charlie Chaplin. Both memories deliver the same fact, but the first is *just* a fact, whereas the second type clothes the information in the rich drapery of sensation and emotion.

Like episodic memories, semantic memories are distributed throughout the brain (see "Weaving the web," pages 32–33). However, the "hook" that triggers their recall is located in the area of the brain that is devoted to language, which in most people is in the left hemisphere, around the ear. This is because language is the frame in which people hold factual information. We have many ways of knowing things – instinct, "hunches," routine actions and emotional responses are all types of knowledge – but facts are pieces of information that you can unequivocally *state*.

Although episodic and semantic memory are treated as separate categories, it is likely that they are very closely related since semantic memory is the core piece of information that is left when the context in which it is learned (the episodic memory) has faded away. In most cases, semantic memories are formed by a number of experiences – millions, perhaps – in which the fact it consists of is reconfirmed. For example, the knowledge that a "roller-coaster" involves traveling in a small car at high speed along rails that dip and climb at terrifying angles may first have been learned during a wildly exciting – and thus memorable – visit to an amusement park. The word would therefore have initially been part of a rich episodic memory. In the years since that event, however, the word "roller-coaster" will have been heard in dozens of contexts, each of which is unique. Think of these experiences as a series of faintly drawn diagrams, each on a separate piece of tracing paper. The only thing that is repeated on each sheet of paper is the meaning of the word "roller-coaster." Now imagine placing the sheets on top of each other so that all of the "roller-coaster" elements are perfectly aligned. When you look at the stacked papers, the "roller-coaster" will stand out while all the peripheral information will be faint. Place the pile in sunlight for a few years and the fainter areas will fade while the roller-coaster part will endure. The same thing happens with semantic memories – they last longer than most one-off episodic memories because they are usually duplicated.

The hippocampus and semantic memory

Brain imaging makes it possible to see the brain at work – tracking the ebb and flow of electrical signals, or the flow of blood to different areas of the brain. Studies of the hippocampus show it becomes active when semantic memories (a list of words, for example) are encoded. But when the memories are subsequently recalled it does not become active. Instead, semantic recall lights up the "word" storage area in the left hemisphere. This is probably because the list is originally learned as an episodic memory, complete with sensory context, which requires the hippocampus to fire up the sensory areas of the brain. For example, in the case described above, the person learning the word list was conscious of their surroundings (the laboratory, researchers, other volunteers and so on). By the time the memory is recalled, however, it has been extracted from its context and is simply a "fact." The hippocampus does not therefore need to re-light the sensory context in which it was originally learned. If someone was asked to remember not just the word list but also the circumstances in which they had first heard it, the hippocampus would probably spring back into action.

Routine activities – working memory

Every waking moment your brain is making thousands of computations that guide your actions. Some of them involve second-by-second actions, while others are long-term plans. Take something very simple: making a cup of tea. You have the main "plan" in mind – to have the drink – and it has to remain in your mind throughout the time it takes to carry out all the little actions needed to complete it. You have to get out the cup, put on the kettle, choose a teabag and so on. Within these "sub-plans" there are smaller components yet: you have to remember which cupboard the cup is in and how to open it, how to pick up the kettle and take it to the sink and so on. And there are even more subsidiary parts than these: how to move your legs to walk to the cupboard, lift your hand to the handle and so on. Like a nest of Russian dolls, there are always actions within actions.

The memories of what has to be done at each level, and how to do them, have to be "kept warm" until the act is completed. If you were making a cup of tea and the memory of one of the necessary sub-plans – the "how-to" memory of opening a box, for example – suddenly dropped out of mind, you would find yourself holding a box of green tea with no idea how to get into it.

Some of the action routines required in a task such as tea-making are unconscious and are carried out more or less automatically, like opening the cupboard. Others, though, need to be kept "in mind" the whole time. Working memory is the name for the part of the brain system that does this, so essentially working memory embraces all the items of knowledge that are active at the time.

Working memory is situated in the front of the brain and consists, it seems, of three main components. There is a tiny spot – not much bigger than a penny – that holds the main plan in mind, and calls in the information

Just another fact

 A couple of years ago I was reading a bedtime story to my four-year-old daughter and came across the word "kangaroo." "Do you know what a kangaroo is?" I asked. "Yes," she said. I was surprised, and wondered if she was just saying that, so I asked her what it looked like. "It stands on two legs and has a baby in its tummy," she said. I asked her how she knew this and she told me her friend, Sally, had shown her a picture of one a week or so before. Then she said: "How do you know what it is?" Of course, I couldn't answer – I just *knew*, as you do.

A couple of weeks ago we were at the zoo and there was a kangaroo. I remembered that little event from a couple of years ago, and said to my daughter: "You know what that is, don't you? Sally showed you a picture of one." She looked at me witheringly. "Of *course* I know what it is. *Everyone* knows what a kangaroo is." Then she gave me a puzzled look and said: "Who's Sally?" She had forgotten the moment she first learned about kangaroos, obviously – even forgotten the little girl who had told her about them. It wasn't an "event" anymore – it had become just another fact.

Jennifer, 32

needed from the rest of the brain in order to complete the task. This is known as the central executive. In addition to this, there are two neural loops that keep the main components of the plan conscious by repeating the pattern of activity that matches them. One of these holds verbal information, while the other holds visual information. These loops are like "scratchpads" or dry-erase boards – the information they hold stays intact until it is erased by the next incoming piece of information. If the item is very important it will be relayed to the hippocampus for processing into a "real" memory, but if the information is the routine "pick up tea cup" it will simply disappear and be replaced by something else.

The "scratchpads" of working memory are conventionally thought to hold between five and seven items, although some experiments suggest it is only two or three. This very short-term memory capacity is thought to be related to intelligence. In the same way that a computer with a larger working memory can crank through problems more quickly, people with a greater capacity for holding images in their heads are expected to have better reasoning and problem-solving skills.

How long does it last?

Working memory holds concepts for only a limited amount of time – about 30 seconds. Meaningful information – that is, things that are important or emotionally significant – tend to be sent to the hippocampus for processing to long-term memory. But "boring" things, like a random string of numbers, will fade within about 30 seconds unless the person deliberately repeats them or uses some outside recall aid such as writing it in a notepad.

"How-to" knowledge – procedural memory

So far we have mainly talked about "declarative" memories – the ones you can bring to mind consciously and talk about. But memory comprises much more than that. We also have a vast store of learned information that is not conscious, but which we would be lost without.

One type of unconscious memory is procedural memory – the "how-to" knowledge that allows us to make the physical movements we have learned. Human babies – unlike most other animals – are born with a very limited repertoire of physical skills. They therefore have to *learn* to walk, talk, manipulate objects, feed themselves and all the millions of other day-to-day physical acts that, as adults, we usually take for granted.

Certain physical activities – such as walking, picking things up and dancing – are "in our genes," in the sense that we are primed by evolution to do them. They are, if you like, a "species memory" that is passed down through the generations. Each individual nevertheless needs to practice these things in order to perfect them. Other physical skills, like playing a piano, driving or typing, need to be learned with great deliberation, because we do not have a genetic program to help us along.

Procedural memories are created and stored in a different way from declarative memories. Conscious perceptions, as we have seen (see "Raw materials," page 18), are constructed along an "assembly line" in the brain which feeds in the raw material of declarative memory. But that assembly line is only one of many. A different assembly line carries information through another part of the brain – the parietal cortex – where it is used, *unconsciously*, to guide our bodies to act appropriately. For example, information coming from the eyes about a cup in front of us will be turned into an *image* by processing along one assembly line, but at the same time the information will be used – unconsciously – to prepare our

The putamen and procedural memories

The putamen is connected by a complex bundle of nerves to the premotor cortex that in turn sends messages to the motor cortex, which instructs the body to move.

Procedural memories – such as riding a bicycle – are held in the putamen. When they are triggered (by getting on a bicycle, for example), they "feed" up to the brain areas that cause the body to move. All of this is done unconsciously. However, the smooth operation of body memory can be interrupted by messages coming back to the motor cortex from the conscious parts of the forebrain. When you undertake a new skill these conscious instructions are essential.

It is only by repetition that the conscious brain can bow out and let the putamen get on with the business of sending instructions. Once we have learned a skill we generally perform it more efficiently when it is left to these unconscious memories. If you suddenly start thinking about where you are putting your feet while you pedal a bike, or how you are balancing on the seat, you are likely to wobble or even fall off.

bodies to deal with the cup. Messages will be sent to our hand, for example, to flex in such a way as to pick it up. Most of these action plans – mental representations – are aborted before they can take place, and we remain unaware of them. But if you were to place a very sensitive detector on the muscles of your arm and hand and then look at a cup, the chances are that you would find the muscle fibers used in picking up a cup would contract a little.

If you carry out a sequence of actions consciously – pedaling on a bicycle, for example – many areas of the brain are brought to bear to produce the right movements. However, most of the actions we have learned are not performed consciously. We might consciously decide to take a bike ride, but it is something we know how to do. We do not *consciously* move our feet into the right position, place our weight correctly in the saddle, grasp the handlebars, and so on. We do this automatically, and it is these automatic movements that are procedural memories.

Doing things on "autopilot" in this way is the basis of expertise. It allows us to get on with the routine parts of a task without engaging the thinking parts of our brain, so leaving them free to work out strategic considerations. In the case of a bike, for example, we can think about where we are going and what we need to do when we get there, instead of having to concentrate on the moment-by-moment business of pedaling, balancing the bike, and so on.

Procedural memories are learned, like any other kind of memory, by repetition, and are encoded by changes in nerve cells, similar to those that create declarative memories – that is, memories that can be consciously retrieved. But whereas event memories are laid down and retrieved by the hippocampus, procedural memories are stored in an organ in the brain called the putamen.

Things you don't know you know – implicit memory

If you have ever been struck by a strong emotion – for example, nostalgia, fear or anger – for no perceptible reason, it may well be that something in your surroundings has jogged an implicit memory. These are memories that influence our feelings or behavior, yet cannot be brought consciously to mind.

Some implicit memories are fragments of past experiences that have either lingered after the "main event" has been forgotten, or have become detached from the event they were originally associated with. Sometimes they encode aspects of an experience that the person was not conscious of at the time it occurred.

For example, a person witnessing, and simultaneously laying down the memory of, a car accident may only be conscious of the sight and sound of the vehicles skidding and crashing into one another, because these will be the things that grab their attention. Unconsciously, however, they will also take in the smell of burning rubber – which may be mixed with a background smell of, perhaps, burning leaves from a nearby bonfire. The person may be sucking a peppermint at the time, and although they will be distracted from the taste (and therefore not conscious of it) when they see the collision, the mint taste will be there in the background. And although the witness may not know it their brain may register all sorts of visual details surrounding the central action, much of which may be quite irrelevant – like a nearby mailbox, or the expression on another witness's face.

The surge of neurotransmitters that accompanies the sight of the accident causes *all* the neuronal activity in the brain – including the part processing, unconsciously, the irrelevant taste of peppermint and the smell of leaves – to be amplified and laid down in memory. Later, the person's *conscious* memory of the event may be narrowed to the central action, but a lot of unconscious context will be stored along with it. Many years later, the taste of peppermint might "pull up" the emotional tone of the event without bringing to mind the whole experience. Or the original event may be forgotten, leaving *just* this odd, united remnant of peppermint and horror. As people get older and accumulate more and more of these unconscious links, their emotional reactions to sensations become increasingly idiosyncratic. Many otherwise inexplicable likes and dislikes may be accounted for by these deeply buried context-dependent memories.

Event memories and context

The contextual elements surrounding event memories can be both beneficial and disturbing. They can be helpful in aiding recall because when one part of a memory is retrieved, it often brings out all the rest. This is why the police often stage a reconstruction of a crime in the original location, at the same time of day, and using lookalike victims. Witnesses who may not consciously remember seeing the incident may be prompted to recall it by seeing the replay of the context in which it took place. The more "rounded" and complete the context in which an incident is recalled, the more likely a person is to remember details. Crime investigators sometimes employ a technique called the "cognitive interview" in which eyewitnesses are encouraged to "tell all" regardless of its apparent importance. For example, a police officer interviewing a bank clerk who has seen a raid will be invited to describe their journey into work, what they were wearing – all sorts of peripheral events that would normally be regarded as irrelevant. They would then be asked to tell their story in a different order – from back to front, perhaps, or describe it in a series of non-sequential episodes. And then they may be invited to imagine how it might have looked from a different vantage point. The bank clerk, for example, might be asked how she thinks the raid would have appeared to someone passing by the window, or what might

In controlled laboratory studies it was found that after only a few hours of instruction in cognitive interviewing technique, police investigators were able to gain as much as 46 percent more detailed information from victims and witnesses than they formally obtained using standard police interviewing. With advanced training and practice they were able to improve information gathering by as much as 96 percent.[1]

have been captured on a video camera looking down from the ceiling. By expanding and juggling the memory of the central event, little details often occur to the witness that otherwise would be eclipsed. On a more mundane level, placing a person "in context" by recalling where you last saw them can aid the retrieval of other facts about them, like their name.

Edouard Claparede

An excellent clinical example of implicit memory was published in 1911 by French physician Edouard Claparede. Claparede repeatedly visited a patient with amnesia and, each time, the patient had no recollection of their earlier meetings until Claparede held a pin in his hand one day as they shook hands. The patient felt the pinprick but, when they next met, still had no conscious recall of their earlier meeting. However, he was somehow inexplicably reluctant to shake hands with Claparede.

The priming effect

We lay down implicit memories all the time, but usually they last for a very short time and do not therefore affect long-term behavior. If you rapidly show a person a sequence of photographs of strangers' faces, for example, then later show them a second sequence that contains some, but not all, of the first images, the person looking at them will have a slightly different physiological reaction to the pictures they have seen before even if they do not consciously recognize them. This is true even if the previously seen faces were flashed up so quickly that the observer did not have time consciously to register them. This unconscious familiarity is known among experimental psychologists as "the priming effect."

Smells are particularly effective triggers of associated memories. Volunteers who memorized a string of words in a room filled with the scent of roses were later found to perform up to 20 percent better when recalling the words in the presence of the same perfume than when asked to recall them in an odorless atmosphere. (See also "State-dependent memory," page 91.)

The white rabbit

 When I was three I went to stay for a while with my cousins in the country. I can't remember the house, or the garden, or anything much, and I only know about it because my mother mentioned it a few times. Then, quite recently, I went past a pet shop and there was a white rabbit in a hutch just outside the door. As I passed I got a whiff of hay, mingled with the smell of rabbit droppings – and suddenly I had this intensely clear memory of helping my cousins to clean out the hutch and feed their rabbit. The funny thing was that at the same time I felt overwhelmingly sad. When I got home I called my mother and told her what I had experienced. She confirmed that my cousins had owned a rabbit. And she was not surprised I remembered feeling sad – it turns out I was sent away to stay with my cousins immediately after my father died because my mother was so upset. Until then I had no idea that I had any memory of my feelings about losing my Dad. I can barely remember him, and whenever anyone has asked me if I remember him dying I've said I can't recall it at all. It took a rabbit to bring it back – of all things.

James, 23

4. Making strong memories

"An impression may be so exciting emotionally as almost to leave a scar upon the cerebral tissues ..."

William James, 1890

Paying attention

Implicit memories, which cannot be consciously retrieved, are often formed by accident, but the memories that you consciously recall later are those that you attended to when the events first occurred. This is because attention amplifies the neural activity that produces the physical changes that make up the memory "traces."

The brain originally developed as the body's alarm system, and attention can be thought of as a special mechanism that the brain has evolved to ensure that we are at our most efficient when danger is about. It "concentrates" brain activity in those areas that deal with the elements of the environment that are most important for our safety.

So, for example, if you are lying in bed one night and hear a creak on the stairs, your brain immediately stops processing everything else – the words of the book you are reading or the thoughts you were thinking – and cranks up activity in the cells of the auditory (hearing) center. This heightened activity allows them to extract every bit of meaning from the creak, to help work out whether it is a burglar creeping upstairs with a knife or the cat trotting up to keep you company.

Such "hotspots" of brain activity are the ones that are the most likely candidates for being laid down in long-term memory. Of course, if the rustle does turn out to be the cat, your attention will shift and the momentary flare-up of neuronal activity will leave no mark. If the creak is followed by the terrifying experience of encountering an armed burglar, however, the whole event – from the creak onwards – is likely to be permanently laid down as a vivid episodic memory.

Attention of this sort is automatic – it is "captured" rather than deliberately applied. But many of the things we want to lay down in memory are not so arresting. There is nothing immediately threatening, or obviously rewarding, about a four-digit PIN number, but it may be very important to remember it. So when you are faced with a learning task like

A passion for football

 I could never pay attention in class. The only time I came to life at school was when we played football – it was my passion. The teachers more or less wrote me off as stupid because I didn't take in anything I was taught, and I failed my English exams. But one year the local paper had a competition for kids to write a report of the local team's winning game against the neighboring town's team. My English teacher persuaded me to go for it. Of course, I remembered the details of every touchdown, the names of every player, more or less every play. I just had to replay the game in my memory – just like a video – and write down what I saw.

I won the competition and started to send in occasional sports reports. Eventually I got a job as a sports reporter and now I can plaster the walls with awards.

Nowadays I sometimes wish I'd paid attention in school because I would like to write about other things. But I'm not sure you can force it. The thing about football was that it *grabbed* me. If you ask me, attending isn't something you *do*, it's something that happens to you.

Roger, 53

remembering your PIN number, you attend to it deliberately. Some people find this much more difficult than others. Although most people can generate attention for long enough to learn something like a PIN number by repeating it frequently, children (and adults) with attention deficit hyperactivity disorder (ADHD) (see page 79 for example) are unable to keep their attention focused.

Emotion

Do you remember your first kiss? The day your granny died? Where you were when JFK was shot, like Daniel Schacter (see the quote, right) or how you heard about the September 11 attacks? The chances are you do, because events like these tend to be accompanied by intense emotion, and emotional memories tend to be the strongest memories of all.

One reason for the strength of these memories is that emotional things make you more attentive, and thus produce more activity in the brain, which, as we have seen, automatically "selects" items for memory storage. They also tend to be unusual events, which again make them good candidates for remembering because these are things we tend to go over and over in our minds.

In addition to this, though, emotion brings about chemical changes in the body, and these encourage the cellular "linking" that turns short-term memories into enduring ones. Intense fear, for example, may result in traumatic flashback memories or panic attacks (see page 90), while powerful feelings of affection encourage memories that consist of feelings of familiarity rather than specific events.

Emotion doesn't only encourage the laying down of events – being in an emotionally aroused state helps us to memorize facts, too, as psychologist Kristy Nielson of Marquette University in Milwaukee, Wisconsin, demonstrated. Nielson asked 32 people to memorize a list of words, such as "fire," "queen" and "butterfly." Half of them then watched a film that

"The true art of memory is the art of attention."

Samuel Johnson

"I do not remember much of what happened just before or after the stunning announcement, but an image of the moment when I first learned the news has remained fixed in my mind for over thirty years. For many of us, the memory of that November afternoon in 1963 feels as though it has been frozen forever in photographic form, unaffected by the ravages of time that erode and degrade most other memories."

"Emotional Memories – When the Past Persists," from *Searching for Memory*, **Daniel L. Schacter, M.D.**

featured a full dental extraction, complete with blood and screeching drill. "It was nasty – it made your skin crawl," she says.

When tested 24 hours later, the traumatized subjects' word memory was around 10 percent better than that of those who'd sat through a dull video on tooth brushing. Emotion helps us to remember, concludes Nielson, "but it doesn't have to be [personally] meaningful."

Correlation of emotions and memories

Any strong emotion encourages the brain to "lay down" whatever it is registering at the time, but different types of emotion help to produce different types of memories.

Emotion	Brain chemical	Memory
Excitement	Acetylcholine and noradrenaline	Vivid event memories or "snapshot" of event.
Pleasure	Dopamine	Vivid event memories or "snapshot" of event.
Disgust	Glutamate	Associative memories such as an aversion to a particular food.
Love	Oxytocin	Increases familiarity with loved object. Released during childbirth to bond mother and child, and during sex, to bond couples sexually. Inhibits the lay-down and recall of traumatic memories.
Fear	Cortisol	Helps create "fear" memories in the amygdala, while inhibiting the lay-down of non-fear memories by the hippocampus.

Part Two
Memory problems

1. Forgetting

"The existence of forgetting has never been proved:
we only know that some things don't come to mind
when we want them. "

Friedrich Nietzsche

Memory and age

Nietzsche's aphorism on the previous page gave rise to the persistent and rather unsettling idea that each one of us carries around a record of our entire lifetime's experience. A complete replay would be possible, if only we could find the right "file" when we wanted it.

That is not true, except in a few quite extraordinary cases (see page 69). For most of us, only a tiny fraction of experience is even selected for consciousness, and just a fraction of that for long-term memory storage. So it is not surprising that we so often draw a blank when we try to remember something.

Generally, though, it is not the things that we failed to make into memories that we search to recall. Rather it is those things we can *half remember* – the name that is on the tip of our tongue; the item we know we came out to buy but can't for the life of us identify as we stand among the supermarket shelves; the "safe place" where we left that crucial document.

Memory "failures" of this sort tend to get worse with age, as memory tests confirm. Most of these tests rely on asking people to do things like repeating a list of words, or recalling concrete details of recent events. Under these, rather artificial, conditions, younger people invariably do better than the old. But as far as actually using memory to understand the world – which is, after all, its primary function – older people may actually do better because they have a richer store of memories to draw on.

Neuropsychologist Brian Levine of The Rotman Research Institute at Baycrest Center for Geriatric Care and the University of Toronto, Canada, studied 15 healthy younger adults, aged 19–34, and 15 healthy older adults, aged 66–89.[1] Participants were asked to choose events from five periods of their lives, ranging from early childhood to the previous year, and recall as many details about the event as possible. In addition, the participants were prompted to stimulate the memory process, by the researchers, who said things such as "That would have been the year you left school."

It was found that the younger participants were consistently better at recalling specific details that were "internal" to the event, or directly related to the event itself. But older participants were significantly better at recalling "external" details, or memories about other factors that were important but may have had little to do with the event itself. "They tended to include less detail and more general factual information that doesn't so much relate to the specific event but relates to extended knowledge," said Levine.

This difference could be characterized as "wisdom." Levine suggests that our memories may have evolved to be like this during our days as hunter-gatherers. "The young males needed to remember specifically how to thrust that spear, or which tree to climb up if they missed. But they relied on the elders to know where the prey was most likely to be found at that time of the year, based on memories of past events that went far beyond the events themselves. Our memory banks may still be useful, even if we have a little more trouble logging on. Some of the details might not be available anymore, but there is a rich fabric woven from the threads of our lives, and those memories may be just as important as the details. "

The change in memory reflects a more general shift in "cognitive style." As the brain ages it seems that it shifts its workload to distribute it more evenly across both hemispheres, such as how we tend to start using both arms to lift heavy objects rather than just one, to compensate for weakening muscles.[2]

Memory failure and compensatory strategies

Most people get worse at some types of memory tasks as they age, but most also develop compensatory strategies that may allow them to function in the "real world" as well, or even better, than those who are younger. Tasks that older people typically find more difficult include:

- Attending to a specific thing (for example, learning a list of facts) without being distracted
- Learning new things
- Retrieving names and words on demand
- Recalling details of past events clearly.

By way of compensation older people tend to be better than the young at:

- "Making sense" of new information by placing it in a meaningful context
- Finding alternative words or phrases for a forgotten word
- Using memories of a specific situation to draw general conclusions.

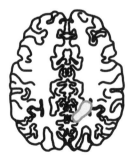

left hemisphere (seen from below) processes the Ds, or detail

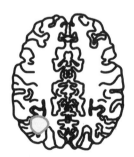

right hemisphere (seen from below) processes the L, or the "bigger picture"

Changes in thinking style

The change in memory skills with age mirrors a more general difference in the thinking style between older and younger people. Brain imaging studies show that the elderly are more likely to draw on both brain hemispheres to solve a task, while younger people use only the brain area that is best suited to it. The two hemispheres are specialized in that the left hemisphere is better at perceiving (and thus recalling) details, while the right hemisphere looks more at the whole situation. These scans show the difference in brain activity when a person is concentrating on the L in the image and when they are considering the Ds (details). In the first case, activity is confined to the right hemisphere, and in the second it shifts to the left. Bringing both hemispheres to bear on a problem therefore helps a person to see a "broader" image.

"Perfect" recall

There *are* people whose memories are so "perfect" that they cannot translate them into useful knowledge. A small number of people known as autistic savants, for example, have the extraordinary ability to recall things they have experienced – the sight of a building, the sound of a tune, a page of a book – in such detail that they can reproduce them perfectly years later. Yet they seem unable to *use* the knowledge they have stored: the autistic artist can draw every brick in a building they once saw, but cannot design a new one; the autistic pianist can play a tune note-perfect after a single hearing, but cannot use the melody as a springboard for composition; the word-perfect reader cannot see the meaning of the story. Memories need to be "fuzzy" for them to be applicable to new circumstances and therefore to act as a guide in a world where we never experience exactly the same thing twice.

The South American writer Jorge Luis Borges wrote of a character, Funes, who had a memory that was so perfect that he could recall the exact shape that the clouds had been in on particular mornings, and could compare these shapes with other objects in his memory such as the veins in the marbled binding of a book. He could also reconstruct entire days of his life. But the memory didn't stop at objects, instances or words. Funes remembered every time he had perceived or imagined anything, so that even remembering the events of the day before would take as long as the day itself. Borges surmised: "He was, let us not forget, almost incapable of general, platonic ideas. It was not only difficult for him to understand that the generic term 'dog' embraced so many unlike specimens of differing sizes and different forms; he was disturbed by the fact that a dog at three-fourteen (seen in profile) should have the same name as the dog seen at 3:15 p.m. (seen from the front). His own face in the mirror, his own hands, surprised him on every occasion. "

The story of Funes has its counterpart in real life: for 30 years the celebrated Russian psychologist Alexandr Luria studied a mnemonist (a memory expert) named Solomon Veniaminovich Shereshevsky, usually known just as "S." Shereshevsky could recall lists of numbers that he had memorized decades earlier, and was actually unable to forget the lists he had memorized while performing as a mnemonist. He could also memorize nonsense syllables, a challenge specifically designed to thwart mnemonic associations.

Shereshevsky also experienced synesthesia, responding to stimulation of one sense with a perception in one or more different senses. For example, he could see sounds and feel their taste and texture. But Shereshevsky's memory was as disabling as it was remarkable. Luria concluded his study by saying: "Each attempt [S made] to move to some higher awareness proved arduous, because at each step he had to contend with superfluous images and sensations. There is no question that his [way of] thinking had both its high and low points."

Second childhood?

Although we have seen that memory can decline with age, it is not actually the very old who have the worst memories, but the very young. Until we are three or four things happen and, exciting though they may be at the time, they just don't stick in our memory. Can you remember anything at all before you were three? Most people can't.

Given what we know about how memories are made – the importance of emotion, excitement, novelty and attention – it seems strange, at first thought, that children should fail to remember all the thrilling things that happen to them in their first few years of life. It is especially odd when you think of how good they are at *learning*. Toddlers learn hundreds of new words a day – far more than an adult trying to learn a new language could achieve. They learn to stand, walk, run and play elaborate games with dizzying ease. So why do they not learn the most important thing of all – what has actually happened to them?

The reason is that autobiographical memory requires a very particular skill – that of "placing" an abstract version of themselves within the events that are being recalled. When you remember an episode from your life you know it was something that happened to *you* because, along with the sights and sounds, is a sense of "being there." Your past self is part of the memory, and the feeling it gives of "being there" is what makes autobiographical memory distinct from, say, a memory of a film you once saw. Very young children cannot create this type of memory because their brains have not matured sufficiently to form the necessary "model" of themselves. Events may be laid down *unconsciously* (though probably not in the way or to the extent that is popularly imagined) but they cannot be recalled at will.

One reason for failing memories in older people may be that, in a way, their brains become a little like those of infants again. The frontal lobes are the most susceptible to (non-Alzheimer's) age-related degeneration and this

"Every man's memory is his private literature. "

Aldous Huxley

may make older people less able to lay down new autobiographical memories. Degeneration is not, for most people, inevitable, however. Brain tissue is similar to muscle in that the more it is used the healthier it stays. Hence the importance, with increasing age, of mental exercise.

The prefrontal cortex

The ability to conjure up a "you" that is not actually right here and now depends on the part of the brain that distinguishes us most from other mammals – the prefrontal cortex. This area in the front of the brain was the last part of the brain to evolve, and in individuals it is the last part to mature. It is the area that combines current perceptions with past memories to make judgements and decisions. In doing this it produces a "model" of the world in which we place ourselves and that we then use to guide our actions, rather as we use a road map to plot a journey.

The right prefrontal cortex is more involved in producing autobiographical memories – that is, ones that include a sense of "self." The left prefrontal cortex plays a greater part in producing memories that do not contain this "personal" element.[3] Therefore when a person "recognizes" an image of themselves, the right prefrontal cortex is activated, whereas an image of another face, however familiar, does not produce activity in this part of the brain.

Selective forgetting

Memory, as we have seen, is not a single system, but several different sub-systems that interact (see pages 38–39). Each sub-system uses slightly different parts of the brain, and this modular arrangement means that one type of memory may be seriously impaired while another is untouched. For example, damage to the hippocampus may prevent a person from laying down memories of new events, while leaving their memory for distant events untouched. Damage to the face-recognition area of the brain (see page 80) may render a person incapable of recognizing even their partner or best friends, but it may not affect their general memory ability. Certain types of words – those defining living things, for example – may be lost while all other words are retained. In one case a woman patient lost her knowledge of "concrete" words (those words that have a solid, real referent), while maintaining an excellent memory for abstract ones. Her responses, when asked to define a list of words, were:

- ■ "needle" —> "I've no idea"
- ■ "hay" —> "don't know"
- ■ "arbiter" —> "one who mediates in disputes"
- ■ "goose" —> "an animal but I've forgotten which kind"
- ■ "supplication" —> "making a serious request for help"
- ■ "poster" —> "no idea"
- ■ "satirical" —> "making fun of in a sarcastic way"
- ■ "acorn" —> "I've forgotten"

Any *sudden* loss of a particular "class" of memories suggests some kind of brain injury and should be investigated immediately. But a gradual and slight worsening of one type of recollection may just mean that the person is neglecting to exercise that skill. Each of us has a slightly different way of using our brains – it is what makes us individuals – and so we all have strengths and weaknesses of memory. People who are natural "doers" are likely to be better than others at retaining episodic and "how-to" memories; extroverts are more likely to remember names and faces; while those who are studious are likely to learn and preserve a formidable vocabulary. With age, these tendencies are amplified because habits of thought become more ingrained through repetition. Provided there is no organic disease, anyone can *learn* to remember, and recall, anything, simply by attending to it and repeating it. The trouble is that the very personality traits that make a person "good" at one type of recollection and bad at another also make them less likely to put in the practice needed to rectify their weaknesses.

Where am I?

It is not just a moviemakers' cliché – the words "Where am I?" really do seem to be the first things that most people say when they wake up in a strange place or come around after being knocked out. It is not really surprising because the need to know our place in the world is, literally, one of the deepest instincts we possess. Getting lost is always disturbing, and when it happens in an environment that should be familiar it is even more alarming.

The structure of the human brain reveals just how important spatial orientation and memory is for our species. One whole lobe of the brain – the section that makes up the area under the crown of the skull – is given over to "maps" of our bodies and our position in space. And a sizeable part of the hippocampus is concerned with registering and laying down memory maps of the landscape through which we travel. Damage to either of these areas can seriously affect a person's ability to find their way around. For example, if the "navigation" area of the hippocampus is affected by a stroke or injury, a person may lose the ability to lay down new routes. Memories of places they knew years before, however, may remain quite

Bad at dates

I used to be very bad at dates. Absolutely hopeless – couldn't even remember my own birthday. What I was really good at was people – I only have to meet someone once and, provided I talk to them a bit, I will almost certainly remember them if I meet them again a year or two later. A couple of years ago I decided to put that talent to use by setting up a company that organizes events – big weddings and parties and so on. I kept the business calendar on a computer and I was quite methodical about consulting it before taking a booking. But one day the system went down and people were calling me and asking if I could do an event on this or that date and I had no idea. I had to turn down everyone until I could get back in to the computer.

After that I started keeping a written calendar as well. But I found after a while that I didn't need it. The shock of losing so much business, and feeling like such a fool, must have forced me to take more notice of dates because now I find that whenever I take a booking I keep a practically indelible record of it in my mind. Instead of just being a string of numbers, each date now seems to "stand out" in time – like a shape, almost. It's rather like seeing a road going ahead into the future with various objects placed along it. I didn't start seeing it this way on purpose – it just happened.

Martha, 48

clear because – like other types of memories – in time, the hippocampus shifts them to long-term storage areas in the cortex.

Some people have naturally better memories for places than others. In part this is a matter of habit and training – people whose lives depend on their ability to find their way around vast tracts of land naturally attend more closely to landmarks. But there also seems to be a genetic component. Men, for example, are on average better at navigating than women, and this is not altogether because of cultural differences. Rather, it is probably due to the action of testosterone, which encourages the growth of right-hemisphere brain areas devoted to spatial processing at the expense of left-brain verbal processing areas.

The ability to find one's way around tends to deteriorate quite badly with age. A study that compared the ability of younger (20- to 45-year-olds) and older (65-plus) adults to navigate their way around a "virtual" maze found that older volunteers took longer to solve each trial, traveled a longer distance, and made significantly more spatial memory errors. After five learning trials, 86 percent of the young volunteers were able to navigate the maze without error, compared to just 24 percent of the older volunteers.

These differences, both in natural ability and in age, do not necessarily translate into differences of real *ability*, though, because people with poor "natural" spatial skills often compensate for them by creating different types of mental maps. Women, for example, automatically tend to remember routes by creating a verbal itinerary: ("right at the Black Horse; left at the bridge" and so on), whereas men tend to rely more on visual imagery. Older people of both sexes who find navigating skills declining may benefit from consciously shifting to the "female" strategy of noting landmarks rather than relying on their sense of direction.

Cultural differences
Cultures in which people traditionally traverse huge distances in the course of hunting or fishing are famous for having extraordinarily good wayfaring skills. The Australian aborigines are often given as good examples, as are the islanders of the South Pacific, who navigate their canoes to tiny islands across hundreds of miles of seemingly featureless ocean, without any of the technology used by Western seafarers. This extraordinary sense of direction is considered normal within those cultures – in some of them "not knowing which way is north" is taken as a symptom of insanity. In isolated communities it is quite plausible that a heightened spatial awareness is inherent – after all, ancestors without it would be unlikely to have survived long enough to produce many offspring. However, learning also comes into it. Children in such communities are taught from a very early age to take careful note of visual landmarks that most of us would miss.

Taxi driver experiment

London taxi drivers who have done "The Knowledge" – an intensive study of the city's labyrinthian streets – have a physical "marker" of their huge map store. The back part of the right hippocampus, which records and replays recently acquired knowledge of routes, is measurably larger in the brains of experienced taxi drivers than in the brains of other drivers.

This discovery was made in a celebrated experiment in which taxi drivers were asked to imagine driving from point to point while their brains were scanned. Researcher Eleanor Maguire, of the Wellcome Department of Cognitive Neurology at University College London, explained: "What we got the taxi drivers to do as well was to recall other types of memory that didn't involve any navigation. So what we asked them to do was recall famous landmarks, because we were interested to see whether any aspect of geography or navigation, even static navigation, would activate the hippocampus. So we asked them to describe famous landmarks, like the Statue of Liberty and the Sydney Opera House, and what we found was that the hippocampus wasn't activated during that time. There were other areas that were active, the regions of the brain that we know we're interested in, recalling objects and things like that; but not the hippocampus. It seems that the hippocampus is important for relating information about landmarks together in a sort of mental map of the world."

Where did I put...?

Forgetting where you left your glasses, car keys or a letter is a common – and irritating – occurrence, but it is not a failure that exclusively afflicts older people. Young children are bad at remembering where they placed things too. Children tend to be biased towards thinking that objects are hidden in the same location where they remember finding them before.

One study asked children aged two, four and six to look for hidden objects in a sandpit. Six times in a row the object was buried in one particular spot, and then it was moved to another place for three more trials. To see if the distance between the two locations made a difference, the distance between the two hiding places was varied, and the study looked at how age differences affected the children's results on the tasks.

As expected, the younger children (the two- and four-year-olds) continued to search in the first location no matter how far apart the two spots were. The six-year-olds only made errors when the two hiding locations were 2 inches apart, rather than 6 inches or 9 inches apart. As children get older, then, their memory for a location becomes more precise and is less likely to be influenced by extraneous factors, such as their longer-term memory of a previous location.[4]

Neurologist Matthias Riepe at the University of Ulm in Germany has scanned the brains of 12 men and 12 women as they tried to escape from a three-dimensional virtual reality maze. The men got out of the maze in an average of 2 minutes and 22 seconds, compared with an average of 3 minutes and 16 seconds for the women. The difference in strategies was reflected by the brain activity of the two sexes during the exercise. While both men and women used the right hippocampus while negotiating the maze, only the men used the left hippocampus. Conversely, unlike the men, women used outer parts of the brain called the right prefrontal cortex and the right parietal cortex. Similar differences have also been observed in rats, suggesting that it may be biology rather than experience that is responsible for these gender differences.

I'll never forget what's-his-name...

Recognizing people and putting the correct name to their face is a complicated process. When it works properly it *seems* easy because it happens unconsciously and apparently instantly. But when it fails to work – as it does for us all at some time – you can almost *feel* the grinding of cogs and gears in your mind as you struggle to put a name to a smiling face bearing down on you across the room, or try to recall the face of a person whose name "rings a bell."

To recognize a person fully can involve bringing together a huge number of stored memories, including facts about the person from semantic memory (he runs the company/lived in a penthouse/owns a dog); from their relationship to you (I know him/he's my boss); and from episodic memories (he walked right past me last time we met); and the person's name. At the same time – if the person is familiar – you will produce an emotional memory of them (see below). Most of this, and sometimes all of it, happens unconsciously – you see the person and immediately "know" who it is.

Recognition failures can occur due to a malfunction in one of the parts of the brain involved in this complex process. Usually they happen because the memory of the person wasn't encoded well enough in the first place.

Attention Deficit Hyperactivity Disorder is a condition in which the brain's natural impulse to "scan" the environment for information – flitting attention from one thing to another in quick succession – cannot be controlled. Normally this attentional roaming instinct is inhibited in older children and adults by activity in a particular part of the frontal lobe. This allows them to concentrate for long enough on any one thing to process it to a point where it can be stored as a memory. People with ADHD are unable to do this, so fewer things "lodge" in their memory.

It has been found that women are better, on average, than men at remembering the way people look. Also, they remember the appearance of other women more clearly than that of men.

Golden rules for remembering people

Laying down a memory of a person is much like laying down any other memory – the golden rules are:

- Pay attention to the person and try to be interested in them (not just look as though you are).
- Focus on their name and "play" with it a little. For example, "Is that Stephen with a 'v' or 'ph'?" "Does Jones mean you're Welsh?"
- Link information about them to existing memories. If they say they have a cat named Cuddles, for example, link them to another cat owner and imagine the two people cuddling their respective animals.
- Try to make time in the few minutes after first meeting a new person to "file" them by visualizing them and repeating to your self some salient pieces of information, including their name. Do the same thing, three or four times, over the next few days.

The "face area" of the brain

There is a small patch of cortical cells on the fusiform gyrus (a bulge on the brain just behind the ear) commonly known as the "face area" because in most people it is activated exclusively by human faces. Damage to this area can result in a person failing to recognize even their nearest and dearest. It was previously assumed that the "face area" evolved specifically for face recognition, but recent research suggests it is, rather, a part of the brain that makes fine distinctions – rather like a magnifying glass enhances an image to clearly show details that are fuzzy to the naked eye.

A few people (around 2–6 percent) have particular difficulty remembering numbers because they have **dyscalculia**, the numerical equivalent of dyslexia. Such people cannot make sense of numbers and find any sort of arithmetic difficult. They do not have the normal "intuitive" grasp of one number being greater or larger than another. Usually, glancing at a four-digit number would automatically hint that it is a "big" number (e.g., 9046) or a small one (0203) and probably acknowledge the zero as a "special" number, and the 2 and 3 as being in sequence. The unconscious registering of certain features means that a great deal of the memorizing is done without even trying. However, a person with dyscalculia would see the string of numbers rather like a line of Chinese ideograms – each one would have to be consciously noted.

Let me introduce myself

 Hi! My name is Bill. I'm 55 years old and I have long gray curly hair and a mostly white beard. I live in San Francisco. If you're like me, it helps a lot to remember what people have said if you have an image of them – all of them, not just the face – in your mind first.

I was born with a condition that makes it difficult for me to recognize faces. There is a small part of the brain that is dedicated to that job, and though it is small, when it comes to recognizing faces, it is very, very good. In me, that part doesn't work, making me blind to all but the most familiar of faces. To help you understand this, let me compare it to two conditions you are probably more familiar with.

People who are "tone deaf" are not deaf to tones. They can hear tones, they just can't tell them apart. People who are "color blind" can see things that are in color. They just can't tell colors apart. Similarly, I can see faces. I just can't tell them apart. The main impact of this is, of course, that I find it much harder to recognize people than most people do. I have my ways, but they are slower and more tedious to use than the face method I lack.

So how bad is it to be face blind? It is a real disability, and its effects on one's life are not trivial. To give you an idea of just how "bad" it is, let me tell you about two things that have happened to me.

Once around midday I met my mother on the sidewalk and did not recognize her. We walked towards each other, and passed within two feet of each other, on a not-too-busy sidewalk in a neighborhood shopping district. The only way I know about this is because she told me about it that night. She was not amused at all by this incident, and she has never forgiven me for it.

Another time I was on a hike with about 20 guys. The group spread out along a trail, and I talked for about half-an-hour with a guy in blue jeans. We parted, and after about 15 minutes I began talking to a guy in red shorts. When I started the conversation with the usual introductory questions, he gave me a strange look and said we had just talked before. I denied having ever seen him before, and mentioned not having talked to anyone in red shorts. He said it had gotten warmer and he had ducked into some bushes to change. And then he recited back lots of the stuff we had talked about half an hour before.

Bill, 55

Amnesia

Total amnesia – when all memories are wiped out – is encountered more often in movies and TV shows than in real life. But people can and do sometimes lose their memories due to brain injury or disease, or as a result of very severe psychological stress. When the organic disease that causes amnesia is progressive and/or untreatable, the memory loss is likely to be permanent. But in many cases amnesia is a temporary affliction that may have no lasting effects.

Amnesia may be retrograde or anterograde. If someone is suffering from **retrograde amnesia**, he or she cannot recall memories that occurred *before* the onset of amnesia. If someone has **anterograde amnesia**, he or she cannot remember incidents that happened *after* the onset of amnesia.

Recognizing someone is a process, most of which is done almost unconsciously. If the procedure is disrupted the conscious mind cannot achieve full recognition, however well they should know the person.

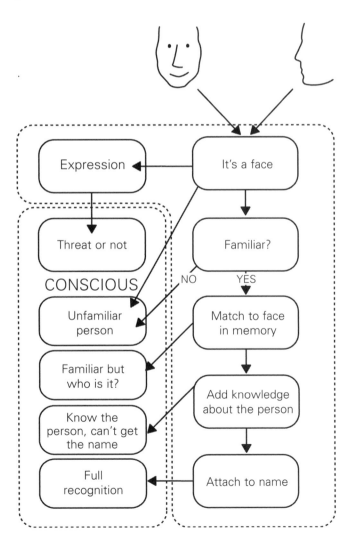

Types of amnesia

Type	Symptoms	Causes and likely outcome
Transient global amnesia	Sudden, short-lasting memory loss and confusion. Attacks can be as brief as 30–60 minutes or can last up to 24 hours. In severe attacks, a person is completely disoriented and may experience retrograde amnesia that extends back several years.	This type of amnesia has no consistently identifiable cause, but researchers have suggested that migraines or transient ischemic attacks (see page 123) may be the trigger. While frightening, it generally has an excellent prognosis for recovery.
Dissociative amnesia (fugue)	Typically, a person with dissociative amnesia suddenly leaves their home and turns up somewhere else a little later with, apparently, no memory of their past life. Short-term and working memory are normal, but they may claim no knowledge of – or very selective memory of – personal events. Dissociative amnesia is sometimes used to refer to traumatic memories that are believed to be "repressed" (see pages 89, 90).	This form of amnesia usually follows an emotional trauma or a period of severe stress. It is considered "psychogenic" – that is, not caused by organic disease or injury. Some people regain their memory within days or weeks, but cases have been reported of people who start completely new lives and never return to their previous identity.
Post-hypnotic amnesia	Inability to recall being hypnotized or to retrieve memories that the hypnotist suggested would be "forgotten." The memories are not permanently lost and may operate unconsciously. For example, a person who was told they would "forget" their telephone number might nevertheless dial it (without knowing why) if invited to dial random numbers.	No one is sure how hypnotic amnesia works. One suggestion is that it is similar to "fugue" in that it arises from dissociation – a sort of partitioning of current perceptions and certain past memories, such that they cannot be brought together. Post-hypnotic amnesia is reversible and the "lost" memories can usually be recalled when the person is rehypnotized.

Korsakoff's syndrome

The person's short-term memory may be normal, but they will have severe problems recalling a simple story; lists of unrelated words; faces; and complex patterns. Episodic memories may also be confused and garbled. The condition may be accompanied by neurological problems, such as uncoordinated movements and loss of feeling in the fingers and toes.

This is due to a deficiency in thiamine (vitamin B1), which causes degeneration of brain tissue. It usually results from alcohol abuse, but may also be due to dietary deficiencies, prolonged vomiting, eating disorders or chemotherapy. Treatment involves replacement of thiamine and proper nutrition and hydration. Drug therapy may also be recommended. However, improvement in memory function is slow and, usually, incomplete.

Traumatic amnesia

Loss of memory for past events following a head injury, especially one in which the person is concussed (temporarily loses consciousness). It usually involves loss of recall of events immediately surrounding the injury, and may last only seconds or minutes. However, in rare cases, it may extend to events that happened weeks or months before. As the amnesiac recovers, he or she usually recalls older memories first, then more recent memories, until almost all memory is recovered.

The amnesia associated with concussion is such that the victim only forgets what happened to them just prior to the head trauma. Generally, the amnesia lasts only seconds to minutes, but in cases of severe trauma, the amnesia may involve weeks to months of the victim not remembering anything. The amnesia gradually gets resolved from more distant to more recent memories. Memories of events that occurred around the time of the trauma are sometimes never recovered.

Amnesiac patient study

The most closely studied amnesic patient is "HM," who was treated surgically in 1953 to relieve the symptoms of severe epileptic seizures. The operation involved cutting out a large part of his hippocampus, which controlled the seizures, but also produced a profound memory deficit.

From the time he woke from the operation HM was unable to lay down any new conscious memories. Day-to-day events remained in his mind only for a few seconds or minutes. When he met someone – even a person he had seen many times a day, year after year – he did not recognize them.

HM believed himself to be a young man, right into his eighties, because the years since his operation did not, effectively, exist for him. When he saw himself in a mirror, he seemed shocked – until the mirror was taken away and the unwelcome sight of his aged faced slipped from his mind.

HM did, however, lay down *implicit* memories in the years after his operation. For example, he learned to play certain tunes on the piano. He did not, however, remember learning them, or even know that he had learned them.

2. Traumatic memories

"Facts of Nature: All forest animals, to this day, remember exactly where they were and what they were doing when they heard that Bambi's mother had been shot."

Gary Larson, cartoon caption, *The Far Side*

Repressed memory

Emotionally traumatic experiences are, by their very nature, likely to be remembered because emotion "amplifies" experience and encourages it to be laid down as a long-term memory. Yet there is also a strong incentive for people to put such events "out of mind," and it seems that the brain has a mechanism that, in some cases, makes this possible. Freud called it "repression" – a "burying" of painful experiences that was so effective that they cannot be recalled except under extraordinary circumstances.

The idea of repression has been strongly challenged in recent years, but something like it does seem to happen in some people who have suffered exceptionally traumatic experiences. These include events such as being involved in combat, getting physically attacked, being caught in an earthquake or flood, being involved in a serious accident, or being tortured, raped or otherwise sexually abused.

Under circumstances such as these – and especially if the victim is helpless – their brain may pull a clever trick: in order to "escape" from the situation, the part of the brain that creates the ongoing sense of "self" disengages or "dissociates" from current events. The terrible sights and sounds and physical sensations that enter the brain are registered, but they are not "bound" into the rest of the memory network. So, although the events may be laid down in neural patterns, they are not consciously accessible.

There are several factors that influence whether a traumatic experience is remembered or whether it is "buried" through dissociation. The type of event and the age of the victim seem to be the most important. One-off experiences (for example, being attacked, raped or witnessing a murder) are more likely to be remembered than traumas that are repeated (domestic violence, continuing sexual abuse or lengthy military combat). Horrors experienced as a result of natural disasters (such as floods or earthquakes) and accidents (plane crashes or fires) are more likely to be remembered than traumatic events deliberately caused by humans (torture or rape). People who are adults when they experience traumatic events are less likely to dissociate conscious memories of the events than children who experience trauma. Research shows that the younger the child is at the time of the trauma, the less likely that the event will be remembered.

Dissociated memories may sometimes be "recovered" spontaneously when a person finds themselves back in a similar situation to that in which the original event happened (see "State-dependent memory," page 91). Sometimes they can be pieced together by conscious effort – although the resulting memory is susceptible to error.

Can "repression" be deliberate?

You can – up to a point – *choose* to forget. U.S. psychologists Dr. Michael Anderson and Dr. Collin Green found that people who deliberately tried to forget certain words had trouble recalling them later. The researchers invited two groups of volunteers to study a list of pairs of words. One group was then invited to "block out" one half of the pairs. Later both groups were shown the words again and asked if they recognized them. The "blocking out" group were worse than the others at recognizing the words they had tried to forget – even when they were offered money as an inducement to recall them.

Brain images of the "blocking out" group showed that during the "forgetting" phase, their brains had generated more frontal lobe activity than that of the control group. This suggests that their conscious decision not to "register" the material inhibited the lay-down process.[5]

The amygdala and psychological trauma

Psychological trauma is registered by an organ in the limbic system called the amygdala that also "stores" bad emotional memories, much as the sensory areas of the cortex store the memories of sights and sounds. The emotion only becomes conscious, however, when the neural activity in the amygdala "passes on" to activate the areas in the frontal cortex that produce conscious thought. The neural traffic between the amygdala and the cortex is two-way, and rather like a seesaw – if activity from the amygdala to the cortex is "heavier" than that coming from the other direction, emotion may overwhelm rational thought. Conversely, if the cortical activity "outweighs" the traffic coming from the amygdala, emotion will be inhibited. Therefore, one way to keep unpleasant memories "out of mind" is to think very hard about something completely different. This deliberate "repression" of disturbing thoughts is difficult to maintain, though, because there are more neural pathways leading up from the amygdala than there are leading down ... we are "wired" to be more emotional than thoughtful. Hence if the amygdala is stimulated to regenerate a particularly strong emotional memory, the activation it "sends up" to the cortex is likely to swamp out thought and may result in feelings of panic and terror that are beyond control (see pages 92–93).

State-dependent memory

If you learn, or experience something, when you are in a certain state of mind or while you are at the same time experiencing a particular sensation, you will subsequently recall it better when you are again in that state. For example, if you read a book on a sunny beach during a vacation, you may appear to forget it completely when you get home. But years later, on another sunny beach, the plot may come flooding back. People with dissociated memories may similarly find that they recall them only when they find themselves in a similar situation.

In one experiment, the results of which are in the table below, volunteers drank an alcoholic or nonalcoholic beverage before studying a list of words. A day later, they tried to recall as many words as they could while either sober or having had one alcoholic drink. Subjects who were in a state of intoxication during both the study and test phases remembered more than those who were intoxicated only during the study phase, demonstrating state-dependent memory.

Retrieval errors in alcohol state-dependent learning

Learning condition	Test condition	Average no. words recalled
sober	sober	14.9
sober	alcohol	10.7
alcohol	alcohol	10.3
alcohol	sober	4.6

Source: Ronald C. Petersen, "Retrieval Errors in alcohol state-dependent learning," *Psychopharmacology*, 1977

Flashbacks

The trouble with repressing bad memories is that they don't always stay repressed. Sometimes they re-emerge in catastrophic ways. Post-traumatic Stress Disorder (PTSD) is a condition in which people cannot quite "forget" some appalling experience. Although they may have "buried" the conscious memory, it recurs in nightmares and sudden memory flashbacks that may seem as vivid and "real" as the original event.

Flashbacks may include sights and sounds that are so intense that they are more like hallucinations. They may ambush a person out of the blue, or be triggered by an environmental "cue." The sound of a firework, for example, may plunge a soldier back into the middle of a gunfight.

Sometimes flashbacks consist only of revisiting the physical state in which the original event occurred. For example, a person who was once traumatized in a gun battle may, years later, hear a car backfire and be reduced to a trembling, sweating, palpitating heap. Yet they may not remember the gun battle at all. All that has been recalled is the bodily state that they were in at the time – a fragment of memory shorn of its context. Because these memories are vivid, frightening and unexpected, they have secondary effects, causing sufferers to doubt their sanity and to fear that they might never recover.

PTSD is very common among fighting forces. It has been recognized, although called by other names, for as long as battles have been waged. It also occurs in people who have

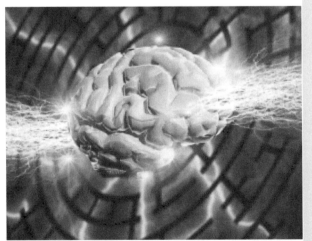

been tortured, sexually abused or involved in accidents and disasters. A national study of American civilians conducted in 1995 estimated that the lifetime prevalence of PTSD was 5 percent in men and 10 percent in women.

Symptoms of PTSD

- Nightmares

- Flashbacks

- Memory and concentration problems

- Jitteriness and over-reaction to ordinary events

- Inappropriate fear and alertness – constantly anticipating danger

- Intrusive memories

- Avoidance

- Being startled at things that most people would ignore, such as a rustle in the trees

- Extravagant reaction to mildly perilous events; a carnival ride, for example, might be treated as though it is life-threatening

Counting out the trauma

This is a simple technique for mastering traumatic memories. It was pioneered by Frank M. Ochberg, who claims that 80 percent of his patients have been helped by it.

Basically all this technique involves is one person (usually a therapist) counting out loud from 1 to 100 while the person with PTSD (the "client") deliberately recalls the traumatic event. As the numbers get closer to the 100 mark, the therapist may invite the client to "come back to the present."   In this, it is a little like hypnosis.

When the counting is finished, the client is invited to discuss the memory. With luck, it will by then be slightly changed by the very act of remembering it while at the same time listening to the therapist counting. This happens because traumatic memories, as we have seen, tend to be "dissociated" from the "web" of experiences that comprise a person's "normal" experience. However, the experience of hearing a counselor counting – a banal, non-threatening, "ordinary" sort of thing – is part of the web. So by remembering the traumatic experience at the *same time* as the therapist counting, the "extraordinary" event is bound to an ordinary one, and so helps to diffuse some of its emotional power. As Ochberg states: "A terrifying, lonely piece of personal history is associated with the security, dignity and partnership of Post-Traumatic Therapy. Future recollection, spontaneous or deliberate, may evoke aspects of therapist and therapy and therefore be less frightening and degrading. "

Being forced to remember an event *in a limited time* is also useful because it puts a natural "stop" on the memory. The person realizes (perhaps for the first time) that they can call an end to it at will.

The central objective of fusing the traumatic memory and the therapeutic experience can be enhanced by "explicit direction." For example, the therapist may suggest to the client, "In future, when you *recall that awful night, you can remember how you turned off the tape at 94, how you heard the counting, how we revisited the scene together.* "[6]

"Phantom" pain

All memories are "phantoms" of a type because they involve the experience of things that are not, strictly speaking, still "there" in the outside world. We take it for granted that sights and sounds can be recalled, but we often find it hard to believe that pain, too, can be a memory. This is probably because sights and sounds can be consciously brought to mind, while it is quite difficult *deliberately* to conjure up an intense recollection of a physical sensation. If you try to recall a physical trauma – accidentally shutting a door on your finger, say – you may be able to produce a shudder, but nothing like the excruciating pain that originally made you scream.

Yet some physical pain *is* memory. The most obvious example is the discomfort frequently felt by people who have had a limb amputated. Phantom limb pains are caused by activity in neurons that would normally receive and transmit signals to and from the missing arm or leg. "Phantom" limb sensation ranges from a shadowy feeling that the missing part is still there, to excruciating pain that appears to come from where an amputated limb used to be. People who have lost an arm or leg in an accident, during which the limb was crushed or trapped, are particularly likely to experience pain. Phantom limb sensations usually fade with time, but in some cases they continue to haunt the person for their entire life.

When a limb is missing, it is, of course, obvious that the pain is a replay of past sensations from that part of the body. But you do not have to lose a limb to experience phantom pain – *any* sensation may be laid down as a memory and later replayed. If you injure your back, for example, the tissues may heal perfectly well, yet you may go on feeling pain, apparently stemming from that area, for weeks or months after the incident. It is impossible to distinguish this pain from one that is caused by ongoing organic damage, so it is very difficult for the person experiencing it to know whether to exercise (the better option if the back is healed) or to rest. Hence the current advice to patients with chronic back pain is to "do as much as you feel you should" – which is not always very helpful.

Like any other memory, "phantom" pain is amplified by repetition. The more you think about it, the stronger and more enduring it is likely to be. But pain is peculiarly difficult to ignore – it is, after all, "designed" by evolution to draw attention. Treatment may therefore include Cognitive Behavior Therapy, which helps to train a person to shift attention from the pain; and antidepressant drugs, which decrease activity in the parts of the brain that monitor and amplify bodily sensation (see also Part Three: Causes and Cures).

Phantom pain:
losing a limb

 I can't remember much about the crash, but I was told that the emergency team took half an hour to cut me free from the wreckage. My arm had been trapped between the bike and the car that hit us, and it had been wrenched up and backwards, as though I was pointing up in the sky behind my back. After the amputation I had a distinct feeling that my arm was still in that position. The feeling went away when I looked at my stump, but if I wasn't looking at it the feeling would come back. At night I would wake up and try to pull it back into place ... then find there was nothing there. Even now (two years later) I still sometimes feel as though I am walking around with my hand in the air. I instinctively bob down when I go through doorways to avoid hitting it.

Jackie, 24

3. Getting it wrong

"The difference between false memories and true ones is the same as for jewels: it is always the false ones that look the most real, the most brilliant. "

Salvador Dalí

False memories

Memories are what we experience when a pattern of neural activity pops up that is so similar to a previous pattern that it creates a partial replay of the original event. These replays are never identical to the original, though. If they were we would not know the difference between the original experience and the memory.

The pattern created by each recall "overwrites" previous memories, so each time an event is brought to mind it is really a *recollection of the last memory* of that event. The slight change created each time something is remembered means that memories gradually change over time. Over the years the actions of people involved in an event may be transposed in memory, so, for example, the sister who threw a glass of water over her brother becomes the one who got soaked. Or an event that happened on one occasion may get transplanted into another scenario – the car accident that took place during a trip to France may be remembered as occurring during a later trip to Spain.

In addition to this gradual alteration in memory, our brains are also capable of laying down memories that are false from the start. This usually happens because an event is misinterpreted. For example, if you expect to see a particular thing, then anything similar may easily be mistaken for it. If a person is told that a house is haunted by a black monk, for example, their subsequent perception of a dark shape in a corner may be "enhanced" by the brain to look like a hooded figure, and the memory that is laid down will reproduce this "sighting" – even if it was just a bathrobe on a hook.

False memories can also be created in the process of recall. If it is suggested to a person that a particular thing happened to them, that person will scour their memory for anything that seems to match the suggestion. They might then retrieve different scraps of memory and piece them together to fabricate a new, false, memory. This will seem just as "real" to the person experiencing it as any other memory.

Eyewitness testimony

 Donald Thomson is an Australian psychologist who has worked extensively on eyewitness testimony. His research showed that witnesses were influenced quite often by something as simple as the clothes the criminal was wearing. If someone else was wearing similar clothes to the offender, they were very likely to be mistaken as the offender. One day Dr. Thomson was picked up by the local police and placed in a line-up. At that time he was picked out by a woman who claimed she was a rape victim of his. What was eventually discovered was that at the exact moment that the woman was being raped, Dr. Thomson was appearing live on television, leading a discussion on eyewitness testimony accompanied by such reliable witnesses as the assistant commissioner of the police. What had in fact transpired was that the woman was raped at the same time as Dr. Thomson appeared on the television, so she did recognize his face, but in no way was he associated with the crime.

The brain's lie detector

You may not know whether a memory is accurate or wrong, but your brain does. A brain imaging study by Daniel Schacter at Harvard University found that the neural patterns produced by a false recollection are different from those that occur when a memory matches an original experience.

While scanning their brains, the researchers asked volunteers to try to recall whether a particular shape had been in a previously viewed group of shapes. When people correctly recognized a shape, the area of the brain that processes visual information was more active than when people mistakenly identified a shape that was in fact only similar. Schacter found a similar effect with word lists, where auditory regions of the brain were more active during accurate rather than false recognition.

The study suggests that, although the conscious mind might make mistakes about what it has seen, the unconscious areas that actually sensed the original are not fooled. They fire only when they are triggered by a stimulus that they have encountered before.[7]

Suggested memory

American psychologist Elizabeth Loftus has conducted experiments that demonstrate how easily the memory can be influenced by suggestion. She has shown that people can be induced to conjure up a memory of an event – for instance, that, as a child, they had become lost in a shopping center – just by being told by relatives that it had happened. Her work has cast witness testimony in a newly skeptical light, and thrown doubt on many sincere, but possibly mistaken, claims of childhood abuse.

The "kidnapping" of Jean Piaget

 Jean Piaget, the great child psychologist, claimed that his earliest memory was of nearly being kidnapped at the age of two. He remembered details such as sitting in his baby carriage, watching his nanny defend herself against the kidnapper, scratches on the nanny's face, and a police officer with a short cloak and a white baton chasing the kidnapper away. The story was reinforced by the nanny and the family and others who had heard the tale. Piaget was convinced that he remembered the event. However, it never happened. Thirteen years after the alleged kidnapping attempt, Piaget's former nanny wrote to his parents to confess that she had made up the entire story. Piaget later wrote: "I therefore must have heard, as a child, the account of this story ... and projected it into the past in the form of a visual memory that was a memory of a memory, but false."

Déjà vu

Déjà vu is marked by a sudden, intense impression of familiarity – people usually describe it as feeling like they have "been here before" or "lived this moment already." It is one of the most mysterious tricks that memory can play.

Déjà vu can happen in any situation. You may be visiting an entirely unfamiliar town, and suddenly feel that you have been right there, in that precise spot, at some other time, even though you know that is impossible. Or you may be talking to old friends around your own dinner table, and feel that you have had this conversation, and lived this moment, before. The feeling goes far beyond any vague sense of having seen or done something *similar* in the past – it is very precise and unmistakable. In a way it is more "real" than a normal recollection, yet it is maddeningly elusive because déjà vu cannot be pinned down to an actual past event. Usually the feeling evaporates within seconds, and cannot be recaptured, however hard you scour your memory.

The sensation of déjà vu is so strange that it has often been regarded as evidence of reincarnation. Another superstitious explanation sometimes put forward is that déjà vu is the memory of a dream in which the person "lived through" the moment in advance of it happening.

Many other explanations have also been put forward: one is that a new situation may sometimes trigger a memory of something similar from the past, but that the recollection becomes confused with the present as it is recalled, creating a sense of recognition without actually bringing the previous event to mind. Freud held that déjà vu occurred when a repressed fantasy of doing or seeing something floated up to consciousness and momentarily imposed itself on real life. Another popular idea is that it happens when the left and right hemispheres of the brain become unsynchronized, so an event is experienced first by one hemisphere, and then, a second or so later, by the other.

Recent brain research suggests that déjà vu may be the result of a momentary error in the process by which the brain constructs conscious perception. Everything we experience is processed along many parallel pathways in the brain. Some of these run through cortical areas and deal with sensory perception (putting visual information together, for example, to form a complete image) and the linking of sensory information to related facts (such as the names of perceived objects and what they are). Other pathways run through the limbic system, and it is here that information is clothed with emotional significance, including, where appropriate, the feeling of familiarity. Normally the information from all these pathways is brought together in the frontal areas of the brain, where it is merged to give the complete picture that forms the stream of consciousness. Sometimes, however, the information flowing along one or another pathway gets held up or blocked, so the resulting experience of an event is incomplete. If a person's emotional pathway is not working properly, for example, they may feel as though people they know well are strangers, even though they recognize intellectually that this is not the case.

Déjà vu may occur when information flowing through the limbic system is "tagged" with familiarity by mistake. A new event does not usually trigger this feeling because the neural firing pattern it creates is not "recognized" as it flows through the limbic system. However, if the limbic areas concerned with memory (around the hippocampus) are for some reason particularly sensitized, they might be provoked into firing by mistake. When this incorrectly labeled information joins up with the information from the cortical pathways, it produces a *feeling* of familiarity that is at odds with the intellectual knowledge produced by the cortex.

Jamais vu

Jamais vu is the converse of déjà vu – instead of feeling familiar with a new situation, it involves feeling unfamiliar in a situation, or with something or someone who really should feel familiar.

Jamais vu may occur, for example, in your own home, or among your own family. Suddenly the furniture, the layout or the pictures on the wall may strike you for a moment as utterly new – it is as though you have never seen them before. Or you may look at someone you have known all your life and, for a split second, feel they are as unfamiliar as someone you have never met. Like déjà vu, jamais vu usually lasts for only a few seconds, and it is probably caused by the momentary failure of the limbic system to react to information appropriately. Damage to the limbic pathway can, however, produce a permanent feeling of jamais vu with regard to people. The resultant feeling of estrangement can be so forceful that people with this condition conclude that their friends and family have been "taken over" by aliens or impostors. This conviction – known as Capgras delusion – can have catastrophic consequences. One man, for example, slit his father's throat, claiming he was "looking for the wires" that he was convinced had been implanted by aliens in his father's body.

Déjà vu all over again

 Ironically, I usually experience déjà vu in situations so similar that they could have been experienced before. For three or four years in a row on Christmas day I'd have a bout of déjà vu sitting around the dinner table with my family. I always knew what was happening – that it was déjà vu, I mean – but that didn't help. Nobody else noticed anything strange. It's sort of like walking around in a dream; you think you know what's going to happen next, and you might be able to change it, but you can't, and what good would that really do? Weird.

Gail, 22

Part Three
Causes and cures

1. Age-related memory problems

"I believe the true function of age is memory. I'm recording as fast as I can."

Rita Mae Brown

The effect of aging on memory

Memory failings can occur at any age. Children are often hopeless at remembering things because they don't attend to them. Young adults may have too much happening in their lives to remember everything they have to do. Some people are naturally poor at remembering names, faces or routes. But it is older people – from the knocking-on-fifty "baby boomers" upwards – that are most concerned about memory loss.

When asked about it, one in two people over the age of 50 say they think that their memory is abnormally impaired, and many of these people worry that this is the start of an inevitable decline into the twilight of dementia. In the vast majority of cases this fear is unfounded. Only about 20 percent of people who report a failing memory are found on formal testing to be unusually forgetful[1] and of those an even tinier proportion – 5 percent or so of over-65s – have symptoms that suggest Alzheimer's disease or some other sort of permanent dementia.[2]

Most people assume that memory gets worse with age, but this is not necessarily correct. Certainly older people tend not to do as well as young adults on simple memory retrieval tests, but such tests are not a very good measure of how well a person's memory functions in day-to-day life (see also pages 66–67). After all, how often do you have to reel off a string of words against a clock? Older people also develop different ways of using their memories – call it a kind of wisdom, if you like – that are often more useful in the real world than simple swiftness of recall.

It is not clear, anyway, that forgetfulness in older people is actually due primarily to their *age*. A large proportion of people with memory problems have physical conditions such as poor eyesight or hearing, diabetes, clogged arteries, mini-strokes and so on, and these are known to increase the likelihood of mental decline. If you examined only those older people who were in very good health, you would probably find very little difference between their memory performance and those of younger people. One study tracked nearly 6,000 very healthy over-60s over a ten-year period and found that 70 percent of them showed no significant decline in cognitive function during that time.[3] So it may be that age-related forgetfulness is due more to our assumptions – including those about ourselves – than to any real change. If you expect to become forgetful because you have ticked off a particular "big" birthday, you are more likely to attribute normal glitches in recall to your age.

Age-associated memory impairment (AAMI)

In the last few years, notable memory decline in the middle-aged and older has been graced with the official designation: "age-associated memory impairment" (AAMI). This new-fangled medical label sounds scary until you realize that it could be attached to at least half the aging population. Rather than regarding it as disease, therefore, it is more useful just to think of AAMI as the identification of a particular aspect of aging – the mental equivalent of crow's feet.

Along with other "natural" aging processes, such as fading eyesight, wrinkles and thinning bones, AAMI is no longer something one just has to accept. There are a few drugs, although currently licensed for other conditions, that may help some people regain sharper memory functions, and specific pharmaceutical therapies are in the pipeline. New findings in cognitive science are honing the age-old practice of mnemonics into a fine science, and research is giving us an ever-clearer picture of how to preserve and/or enhance the brain to promote better functioning.

Quick memory test

If you are worried about your memory, it is worth checking to see if your problems are unusually severe. A full memory assessment requires a battery of psychological and physical tests that can only be carried out by a medical professional. However, this quick test offers a very rough benchmark: if you are of normal intelligence and believe you had a normal memory in the past, your performance on this test will indicate whether you would benefit from a full memory assessment.

1. Write down the month, day of the week and year.

2. Look once only at the words below, then cover them up. When you have finished answering the rest of the questions, write down from memory what they are:
orange, television, cushion

3. Without looking at your watch, write down what time you think it is. Then look at your watch and write down the actual time.

4. What are the names of the last five U.S. presidents?

5. Name the following items:

6. Can you remember the address of the last place you lived?

7. Can you recall what you were doing on each of the previous seven evenings?

8. Have people told you that you repeat yourself in conversation, or have you found yourself doing this?

9. Are you ever aware that people are getting irritated with you because you have forgotten something?

10. Do you ever return from shopping to find you have forgotten an essential item?

11. Do you find it increasingly difficult to follow directions?

12. Do you get lost in places that you have visited frequently?

13. Do you have trouble recalling words, even though you know that you know them?

14. Do you misplace things practically every day?

15. Are your memory difficulties impinging on your work or social life? For example, do you sometimes avoid people because you cannot remember their name?

16. Without looking back, write down the three words you memorized earlier for question 2.

Now turn to page 171 and follow the instructions given there to score your test and see what your results mean.

Normal aging or dementia?

The brain is a physical organ like any other, and therefore subject to degeneration in much the same way as any other part of the body. You can prevent or slow down the process of brain decline by mental exercise, just as you can preserve joint and muscle fitness by physical exercise and healthy living, but change is inevitable.

Medical opinion is divided about whether the dementias – of which Alzheimer's is the most common – are distinct diseases or the inevitable result of age-related changes to brain tissue. Evidence against the idea that they are one and the same is that the brain changes which signify Alzheimer's disease first occur in the hippocampus, whereas those that occur in people who do not go on to have catastrophic memory loss first occur in the brain's frontal regions.[4]

On the other hand, the prevalence of dementia is very clearly linked to age – it affects less than 2 percent of people under 65, while every third person over 90 years of age suffers from it.[5] About half of those affected by dementia suffer from Alzheimer's disease. Symptoms include memory loss, disorientation, personality change and delusion. It ultimately leads to death. It has been proposed that we would all end up with dementia if we were to live to be 150 or more. Certain genes are associated with early-onset Alzheimer's disease, but it may not be that these genes *cause* the illness – rather that others *prevent* it and are lacking in those people who have early-onset Alzheimer's.

Certain specific changes in the brain are "markers" of age-related dementia. In Alzheimer's disease these are "tangles" and "plaques" of dead tissue. Lewy Body dementia (probably the second most common type of dementia) is characterized by the presence of small cysts, while vascular dementia is caused by multiple small areas of dead tissue caused by tiny strokes.

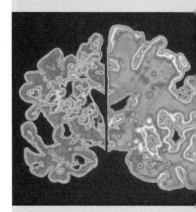

Alzheimer's disease
Brain imaging shows a vertical (coronal) slice through the brain of an Alzheimer's patient (at left) compared with a normal brain (at right). The Alzheimer's disease brain is shrunken due to degeneration and death of nerve cells. Apart from a decrease in brain volume, the surface of the brain is often more deeply folded. Tangled protein filaments (ofibrillary tangles) occur within nerve cells and patients also develop brain lesions of beta-amyloid protein, causing the symptoms described in the text, left.

AAMI and Alzheimer's disease

This table shows the differences between "normal" age-associated memory impairment (AAMI) and Alzheimer's disease.

Activity	AAMI	Alzheimer's disease
Rate of onset	Gradual – over decades, with long periods of stability.	Sudden – often a precipitous decline within months.
Memory	Forgets some experiences, or parts of them. Sometimes recalls them later. Retains memory of very familiar places and people.	Whole periods of life are forgotten and, once lost, these rarely return. Gets lost on routes and in places that should be familiar. May not be able to find way around own home. Fails to recognize family and friends.
General intelligence	Able to follow plans of action or instructions, though may lose thread or need prompting. Able to use memory aids such as written notes. Recall of information retarded, but may be able to arrive at "answer" through indirect route.	Gradually loses the ability to follow written or spoken instructions or to construct and follow through a plan of action.
Language	Unaffected.	Increasing difficulty in self-expression. May talk in a rambling, incoherent manner.
Self-care	Capable.	Gradually becoming incapable.
Mood	Unchanged, except for personal irritation due to own condition.	Unstable mood – may swing from depression to euphoria for no obvious reason.
Social behavior	Remains socially competent.	Behaves increasingly inappropriately.

2. The effects of illness

"A healthy mind in a healthy body"

Juvenal, Roman poet, 55 AD–127 AD

Injury and illness

Memory functions are so widespread in the brain that almost any injury or damage to the organ is likely to cause some sort of memory problem. The precise impairment depends on where the damage occurs. Injuries to the front of the brain, for example, are likely to affect working memory – the ability to "juggle" what is happening in the moment with previous memories in order to make judgements and plan actions. Damage to the parietal lobes, the area beneath the crown of the skull, may cause a person to "forget" how to use their body correctly. An injury to the temporal (side) lobes may affect the storage or retrieval of long-term memories, including words.

Brain damage may be the result of trauma – a road accident, for example – or the damage may arise from disease. Illnesses that may affect the brain include:

Diabetes

People with diabetes sometimes show impairments in certain kinds of memory tasks, such as the ability to repeat a short story from memory (i.e., verbal memory is affected). The precise mechanisms that lead to memory deficits in diabetes are not clear, but it may be because in a person with diabetes, cells in the body – including brain cells – aren't able to obtain sufficient glucose to fuel memory tasks. As a result, sugar levels in the blood may remain high even as cells are "starved" of energy. Or, high blood sugar may have some direct damaging effect on brain cells, especially in the hippocampus.[6]

Diabetes can be controlled by diet when it is mild, or, in more severe cases, by insulin injections or drugs, and research shows that people with diabetes who reduce their blood sugar levels experience significant improvements in working memory. One study showed a 30 percent improvement in short-term recall among people with Type 2 diabetes within six months of gaining control over their blood sugar levels through drugs. The better the condition was controlled, the better the people did on memory tests.[7]

Thyroid gland deficiency

The thyroid gland produces hormones that affect every cell in the body, including those in the brain. These hormones can stimulate and even change the structure of the hippocampus, and they also affect enzymes that regulate the metabolic rate of brain cells.[8] Given this, it is not surprising that thyroid hormone deficiency produces memory impairment. Forgetfulness and absent-mindedness are classic symptoms of hypothyroidism, and may indeed be the only symptom of the condition.[9] Fortunately, memory loss caused by thyroid hormone imbalances can often be effectively treated. However, it can be difficult to diagnose so very careful testing is needed, ideally by a specialist.

Infections

Encephalitis and meningitis are inflammatory diseases of the membranes that surround the brain and spinal cord and are caused by bacterial or viral infection. Once the infection has entered the bloodstream, it can localize in the brain, causing inflammation of the brain tissue and surrounding membranes. White blood cells invade the brain tissue as they try to fight off the infection. In very severe cases the brain tissue swells (cerebral edema) and nerve cells may be destroyed. There is also a risk of cerebral hemorrhage (stroke).

The most common cause of encephalitis is the herpes simplex virus, but it can also be caused by viruses such as influenza (flu), measles, chickenpox and syphilis. Encephalitis can also be caused by a head wound that penetrates the brain and becomes infected, or by infection elsewhere that gets into the bloodstream and is carried to the brain. HIV, the virus leading to AIDS, can also weaken the immune system, allowing various other infections to spread into the brain. Symptoms range from cold-like headache, fever and dizziness to more serious motor dysfunction, paralysis and coma. If the underlying cause is treated promptly, outlook for recovery is generally good; left untreated, encephalitis can cause irreparable brain damage or even death, so it is very important to see a doctor quickly. Most people make a full recovery from meningitis and encephalitis, but neurological symptoms may linger for months, and memory impairment and lack of concentration are very common. In very rare cases encephalitis has been known to damage the hippocampus, producing a form of amnesia where new memories cannot be laid down.

Epilepsy

Memory loss is one of the most common and disabling effects of epilepsy on the brain. Some types of seizure trigger convulsions, whereas others unfold with more subtle signs – a repeated arm movement or facial twitch, for example. Regardless of how epilepsy shows itself on the outside, on the inside the person is undergoing a kind of storm in the brain, one that frequently results in memory loss. Anticonvulsants used to treat epilepsy reduce the severity and frequency of seizures, but they can also impair normal brain function and cause memory problems themselves. This may be because the medication slows the brain down so much that the patient has trouble learning and remembering new information. Usually doctors can solve this problem by finding just the right medication and dose for the patient.

Stroke

One of the most common causes of memory impairment, particularly in the elderly, is a stroke. Strokes are usually divided into three main types: **ischemic**, in which the blood supply to an area of the brain is cut off by a blocked artery, resulting in a shortage of blood to the brain; **hemmorrhagic**, in which a blood vessel bursts; and **transient ischemic attack (TIA)**, often called a "mini-stroke," which is a temporary interference with blood flow to the brain. It may be due to a small blockage that then clears itself, or is too minor to cause significant damage. Often the symptoms – dizziness, loss of balance and perhaps momentary loss of consciousness – are so brief and insignificant that the person does not know they have had a stroke. However, some people have repeated TIAs that cause cumulative damage and eventually result in a form of dementia.

About one in three patients have significant memory impairments three months after a stroke, and in some cases the problem may be catastrophic. If the stroke occurs in the area of the brain concerned with language, for example, a person may at first be bereft of speech, or unable to link objects to words. However, in many cases the problem diminishes with time, due to the brain's astonishing ability to rewire itself. If the language area is damaged, for example, the brain may start to use the corresponding language area in the other hemisphere of the brain for speech.

Depression

Not only does severe depression plunge a person into unrelieved misery, it also restricts their ability to attend to events, to organize their thoughts, to make judgements, initiate tasks and lay down long-term memories. One reason for this is that depression involves a reduction of activity in the frontal cortex that slows down working memory. Indeed, a depressed brain is generally less active than normal. It is partly the lack of "chatter" between the brain cells that accounts for the depressed person's dullness of thought and grayness of mood.

To make things even worse, depression makes it difficult, if not impossible, for a person to retrieve happy or consoling memories. Other people might try to remind them of something pleasant that happened, but the depressed person will only be able to remember it vaguely, if at all. This is because happy memories include an element of the emotion itself. If you recall something cheery, and recall it vividly enough, it automatically perks you up. But depression is, more or less by definition, the *inability* to perk up. Therefore happy memories are not – and cannot be – fully recollected in a depressed state. If they could be, the person would not be depressed.

Long-term memory formation is impaired during a period of depression for several reasons. One is that the person is not interested in anything. Without interest it is very difficult to attend, and without attention it is difficult to experience anything strongly enough to lay it down as a memory. The exception to this is experiences that are sad or frightening. The one part of the brain that is often trigger-sharp during depression is the amygdala, which latches on to, and amplifies, negative experiences.

The other reason is that people who are prone to depression have a smaller hippocampus than others. It is not known whether this is caused by shrinkage due to the stress of depression, a lack of "exercise" (brain "modules" are like other muscles in that the more they are used the bigger they become) or whether it is part of the genetic inheritance that makes certain people susceptible to depression in the first place.

The effects of ECT

 I felt peculiar after the first session of ECT (Electro-convulsive Therapy), and for a day or two I was not really sure what was happening at all. I couldn't work out why I was in the hospital and when I went to call my home I found I couldn't remember my phone number. Things got a bit clearer over the next few days, but I was left for weeks with a funny feeling that there were things I *should* be remembering – but I couldn't work out what they were. I had the treatment six months ago – a series of five, and each one left me feeling like this but for shorter periods. That whole period in the hospital is very vague now, though whether that is because of the treatment or just that I wasn't really able to take anything in at that time, I don't know.

The growing brain

Until recently, it was assumed that once a brain was mature the number of nerve cells in it was fixed for life. This is now known to be incorrect – new cells are "born" the whole time. Many of them, however, perish because they cannot find a place in the cellular "network" where they can function. Neurogenesis, the development of new nervous tissue, has been shown to occur in the hippocampus, and in other primates it has been detected in cortical tissue too. Scientists are now working on ways to stimulate the growth of new cells in damaged brains, and to help them wire into the existing network in such a way that they can "fill the gaps" caused by injury or disease.

ECT and memory

Severe depression is generally treated with antidepressants (see pages 134–37), which are effective in about 75 percent of cases. However, a person with very severe, unremitting depression may be offered Electroconvulsive Therapy (ECT). ECT involves inducing a controlled brain seizure under anesthetic by administering an electrical current to the brain through electrodes placed on the head. It is an effective treatment for depression when all else has failed, but it invariably leaves the person with temporary memory problems, and in some cases certain long-term memories are lost forever.

The importance of sleep

Forget stories of people who function brilliantly on three or four hours of sleep a night. Most of us need at least seven hours in order to perform properly, and chronic sleep disturbance can severely affect memory.

This is because a large part of the "lay-down" and consolidation stages of learning occur during sleep. The details of how it happens are still not entirely clear, but current evidence suggests that during the Rapid Eye Movement (REM) phase, which is associated with vivid dreaming, the hippocampus "replays" recent events, sorting and tidying them up as it goes. Then, in the "quiet" phase of sleep that follows REM, the newly laid-down memories are played back to cortical areas where they are stored as long-term memories.

The "replay" of waking experience is often very fragmented and is mixed up with older memories. The resulting kaleidoscope helps to create the peculiar meandering and bizarre quality that characterizes dream consciousness.

Some memory tasks are more affected by sleep deprivation than others. A recent study, for example, found that recognition memory for faces was unaffected by people who were deprived of sleep for 35 hours. However, while the sleep-deprived people remembered that the faces were familiar, they had much more difficulty remembering in which of two sets of photographs the faces had appeared. In other words, their memory for the context of the faces was significantly worse even though their facial recognition memory was unchanged.

The effects of jet lag

Repeated bouts of jet lag may harm an area of the brain important to memory, according to a recent study in *Nature Neuroscience*. For the study, researcher Kwangwook Cho of the University of Bristol, England, recruited 20 international flight attendants who routinely worked flights crossing seven or more time zones. Such journeys throw off the brain's internal sleep/wake clock, causing sleep disturbance and general stress and fatigue. The flight attendants were all women aged between 22 and 28, with five years of service at various airlines. They were split into two groups, based on how long they had to recover between international flights. One group had a full 14 days, while the other group typically only had 5 days to reset their body clocks. The women were later tested for their memory of a familiar place. The short-recovery group, Cho reports, performed worse than those who had two weeks to recover. Other studies have also shown that flight crews were slower to recall items from short-term memory than those not encountering jet-lag conditions.[10]

Before encoding   After encoding

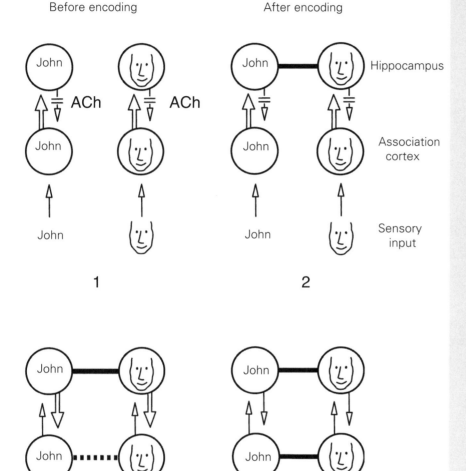

1

2

Memory consolidation during sleep
Memories seem to be consolidated during sleep. A person's name, for example, may be linked in memory with a recollection of their face. This process is thought to depend on the ebb and flow of neurotransmitters in the hippocampus.

A1) During waking, a name "John" and a face are registered and a representation of this knowledge is then fed to the association area and the hippocampus. Acetylcholine (ACh), which is high during waking, prevents the hippocampus feeding the signals back to the cortex, so the information is not distorted or merged with other incoming stimuli. A2) Instead they link together and are "locked" or encoded in the hippocampus.

B1) During non-dreaming sleep, ACh levels fall, and this allows the newly encoded memory to be fed to the association cortex. There is no new information coming into the cortex from outside during this time because sleep imposes a sensory blockade on external stimuli. The feedback from the hippocampus therefore re-triggers neural patterns that were activated during previous waking – including the sight of John, and the neural pattern corresponding to his name. As these two cortical patterns fire in unison, they become linked – and the neuronal linkage forges a new connection between the concepts, such that if one (the face) is triggered the other (the name) is likely to fire up too. Hence in B2) the memory of John's name is consolidated.

3. Drug treatment

"The separation of psychology from the premises of biology is purely artificial because the human psyche lives in indissoluble union with the body."

Carl Jung, *Factors Determining Human Behavior,* **1937**

Treatment for Alzheimer's disease and dementia

A handful of drugs is available for the treatment of Alzheimer's disease and other dementias. Most of them work by conserving or increasing the level of a neurotransmitter called acetylcholine – one of the brain chemicals that is necessary for storing and recalling memories (see page 61). Acetylcholine levels drop when the brain cells that produce it die off. Brain cell death is catastrophic in Alzheimer's disease, but to a lesser extent it is also part of the natural aging process, so acetylcholine decline is common both to dementia and to age-associated memory impairment (AAMI).

These dementia drugs – called cholinesterase inhibitors – do not create new neurons, but they do make more acetylcholine available to those brain cells that remain. They do this by inhibiting the action of an enzyme, cholinesterase, that scoops up acetylcholine molecules from around the synapses – the tiny gaps between the cells. Although cholinesterase inhibitors are licensed only for the treatment of people with diagnosed dementia, it is possible that people with "ordinary" memory problems could benefit from them. Indeed, these drugs might end up proving more useful for enhancing memory in "normal" people than for treating Alzheimer's disease, for which they have proved to be a disappointment.

There is little evidence to support the use of dementia drugs on "healthy" people because all the large trials have been done on the target population of dementia patients. However, a little evidence does exist to back up the notion that they would work on people with normal age-related memory problems too. One study, for example, found that giving Donepezil (Aricept, see opposite) to middle-aged pilots during a flight-simulation exercise significantly improved their performance, particularly their ability to remember things like code numbers and instructions from ground controllers.

Cholinesterase is an enzyme that floats around in the synapse and eats up excess acetylcholine. It breaks acetylcholine down into its constituent parts, which are then carried off in the lymphatic fluid. Cholinesterase inhibitors stop these from working, so the neurotransmitter remains in the synapse and is thus available to do its work of triggering activity in neighboring cells.

The latest drug to be licensed for treating dementia works quite differently from the others. Memantine (see below) targets a receptor on the brain cells that responds to glutamate, the most widespread neurotransmitter in the brain. Glutamate encourages brain cells to fire, and in people with Alzheimer's disease the amyloid plaque deposits that characterize the condition indirectly stimulate the production of excessive

Drugs for Alzheimer's disease and their effects

Drug	Brand name(s)	How it works	Side effects
Tacrine	Cognex	Cholinesterase inhibitor.	Nausea, vomiting and constipation – severe at high doses.
Donepezil	Aricept	Cholinesterase inhibitor.	Nausea and vomiting.
Galantamine Recommended to be taken with food and maintaining fluid intake.	Razadyne	Cholinesterase inhibitor. It also sensitizes neurons to acetylcholine. Effective for dementia caused by mini-strokes as well as Alzheimer's disease.[11]	Nausea (affects 1 in 6 who take it), diarrhea (up to 1 in 8), anorexia and weight loss. Typically these are temporary and occur at start of treatment or when dose is increased.
Rivastigmine	Exelon	Cholinesterase inhibitor. Blocks a form of the enzyme that becomes more important in later Alzheimer's, so may be more useful for severe dementia than mild impairment.	Nausea (affects 50%) and vomiting, especially at start of treatment and as the dose is increased. Weight loss, dizziness and loss of appetite are common.
Memantine	Namenda	Protects brain cells from "burning out" by partially blocking the NMDA receptor (a type of glutamate receptor).	Likely to impair memory function in those who do not have Alzheimer's.

glutamate. This then overstimulates the neurons and causes them to burn out. Memantine is designed to protect the cells against this by partially blocking the effect of glutamate. Although it is theoretically probable that Memantine could help protect people with very early Alzheimer's disease, it is very unlikely to benefit people who do not have the amyloid plaques associated with Alzheimer's. Indeed, in a healthy brain it is likely actually to impair memory by damping down the activity of the brain cells involved in laying down and retrieving information.

Antidepressants

The brain systems underlying memory and mood are intimately linked. Both are regulated by a complex cocktail of fluctuating neurotransmitters, some of which are involved in both systems. Hence memory disorders are common in people who are depressed, and mood disorders are part and parcel of dementia disorders such as Alzheimer's and Parkinson's disease.

Depression is marked by a change in a person's normal brain state that manifests as a wide range of alterations in mood, behavior, thought patterns and physical functioning (see pages 123–24).

Given that depression is defined as a *change* in one's normal state, antidepressants should not, in theory, benefit people who do not fulfill the diagnostic criteria for depression. However, just as there is a large gray margin between "normal" age-related memory impairment and dementia, so there is a gray area between "normal" mood and clinical depression. Some people are naturally "set" by their genes to live in this marginal place. Most of the time they do not qualify as "depressed," but are naturally pessimistic, apathetic or lacking in drive. Such people may have brain chemistry that is similar to those who are diagnosed as depressed, and antidepressants may therefore help them as they do a person who is formally diagnosed as being depressed.

Antidepressants work by increasing (or conserving) the levels of certain neurotransmitters, or by making brain cells more sensitive to them. They do this very quickly – the change in neurotransmitter activity is measurable within hours of taking antidepressants. However, they do not actually benefit a person's mood for some time – anything between ten days and eight weeks.

This odd feature of antidepressants is not understood. One theory, though, is that the change in neurotransmitter levels starts a cascade of chemical actions that results in the growth of new brain cells, and that it is only when these cells mature and start working that the benefits kick in. One region of the brain where new cells have been shown to grow is the hippocampus, the seat of memory.[12] This may explain why improvement in memory is commonly reported by people who are treated with antidepressants.

Some antidepressants, however, seem to work in part by *inhibiting* memories. One of the distressing features of depression is an onslaught of bad recollections and self-demeaning thoughts that are often derived from imagined personal failures in the past. These diminish with successful antidepressant treatment.

The decrease in unhappy memories may be because these drugs encourage increased activity – possibly as a result of new cell growth – in the prefrontal cortex. The effect of this may be to "drown out" the bad memories and allow a person to concentrate on "here and now" information. The net effect, therefore, is to boost working memory, and perhaps to allow access to more pleasant recollections.

The picture is further complicated by the fact that some antidepressants (mainly tricyclics) damp down acetylcholine, the neurotransmitter that enhances attention and excitement. In other words, they have precisely the opposite effect to the anti-dementia drugs that conserve acetylcholine. Not surprisingly, they are also associated with memory impairment.

Classes of antidepressants

Antidepressants alter the level, availability or effect of various neurotransmitters. The main neurotransmitters are serotonin, dopamine and noradrenaline, which are all monoamines. Some drugs target a single chemical, while others work on two or more. The main classes of antidepressant are:

Selective serotonin reuptake inhibitors (SSRIs) such as fluoxetine, citalopram and paroxetine

Serotonin is not directly implicated in memory lay-down or retrieval, but boosting serotonin function generally relieves anxiety. In the short term, anxiety impacts memory by causing people to be distracted from "here and now" information (thus impairing working memory) and to be swamped by bad memories at the expense of being able to recall more positive experiences. Normalizing serotonin function will therefore "free up" a person's brain to function better, with an apparent improvement in memory.

In the long term, normalizing serotonin function may protect memory function by decreasing the production of the "stress" hormone, cortisol. Cortisol directly impairs memory because it targets, and destroys, neurons in the hippocampus, the brain's central memory processor. Studies have shown that chronically anxious people have a visibly shrunken hippocampus – up to 60 percent of its volume may be worn away, over the years, by the effect of cortisol.

In some people, though, increased serotonin function may actually impair memory because its lulling effect on anxiety may also reduce vigilance and therefore make the person less attentive to things that would normally worry them – and thus engage their attention. Indeed, benign forgetfulness of this kind is probably one of the ways in which antidepressants lift mood.

Monoamine oxidase inhibitors (MAOIs) such as moclobemide, tranylcypromine, phenelzine and selegiline

These drugs work by inhibiting an enzyme that breaks down all three monoamines – serotonin (see above), dopamine and noradrenaline – and thus leaves them intact to do their work of carrying messages from cell to cell.

Dopamine is the neurotransmitter that produces motivation and feelings of pleasurable anticipation. It is the chemical that is catastrophically depleted in Parkinson's disease, and low levels are also implicated in depression.

Noradrenaline is a generally stimulating chemical – it produces feelings of engagement and excitement, and increases concentration. As we have seen, our ability to "use" experience (working memory) as well as our ability to lay it down for future recall depends on our paying attention to it. It is therefore plausible that upping the effect of dopamine and noradrenaline enhances memory function, as well as improving mood in a person who is depressed.

MAOIs are generally not prescribed except as a last resort because they sometimes interact dangerously with common foods. However, newer, "reversible" MAOIs (for example, selegiline) do not have this effect.

Tricyclic antidepressants such as imipramine, amitriptyline and amoxapine

Drugs of this type work mainly by increasing serotonin and noradrenaline levels. Most of them also tend to *block* the effect of acetylcholine – the neurotransmitter most closely associated with mental decline in dementia. Hence, unsurprisingly, they are likely to impair, rather than to enhance, memory. The effect does not seem to be lasting, however. A study that traced patients over more than 11 years found no discernable reduction in cognitive or memory faculty among those who had been taking the drugs.[13]

Statins

Statins are drugs that lower the amount of solid fatty compounds floating around in the bloodstream. This is the junk that collects on the inside of artery walls and slows down or blocks the free flow of blood. Statins are usually prescribed to reduce the risk of heart disease and stroke, but it is possible that statins might also help to prevent the accumulation of plaques and tangles in the brain that characterize Alzheimer's disease, and that are also found (though in small amounts) in the brains of people with age-related memory impairment. This seems plausible because Alzheimer's disease plaque contains cholesterol.

Two large epidemiological studies suggest that taking statins could help stave off dementia. In the first, researchers examined the medical records of more than 57,000 patients aged 60 or older at three U.S. hospitals (two of them operated by the Veterans Health Administration). The prevalence of Alzheimer's disease was 60 to 73 percent lower in those taking Mevacor (lovastatin) or Pravachol (pravastatin) than in others.[14] In the second study, 284 people aged 50 or older diagnosed as having Alzheimer's or another form of dementia were compared to similar people without dementia. The risk of dementia was 71 percent lower in people taking statin.[15]

However, despite these impressive results, it is by no means certain that statins stave off Alzheimer's disease. Other (though smaller) studies have shown no evidence that this is the case, so the story is far from clear. Even if they do, it cannot automatically be assumed that they will help people with benign memory or cognitive impairment because, as we have seen, it is not clear whether these conditions are a "mild" form of dementia or something entirely different.

To make things even more complicated, statins are also associated with memory *loss*. Amnesia is one of the side effects listed by the makers of Lipitor, one of the best-selling anti-cholesterol drugs, and many other brands of the same type are reported to have a similar effect.[16]

A study by Beatrice Golomb at the University of California, San Diego, documents at least 100 cases of memory problems among statin users, including 30 cases of transient amnesia. Around 60 accounts of memory problems in patients who had taken statins were also noted by a team from Duke University in North Carolina who analyzed a massive database of drug side effects.[17] In some cases the patients' memory problems disappeared when they stopped using the drugs, but came back when they went on them again. One theoretical explanation is that the drugs reduce the ability of brain cells to signal to one another.

It is therefore quite plausible that statins have two quite different effects on memory: in the long-term they may protect the brain (and thus memory) from the "gumming-up" effects of plaques, while in the short term they may reduce the ability of nerve cells to conduct messages, and so bring about sudden memory lapses.

Transient Global Amnesia

 The particular form of amnesia associated with statin use is Transient Global Amnesia (TGA, see page 83). One apparent victim of this curious side effect is former NASA astronaut and retired doctor Duane Graveline. Graveline had his first attack shortly after starting Lipitor, one of the most common statin drugs, which is prescribed to lower cholesterol. This is his story:

"A few days into the treatment my wife found me aimlessly walking about the yard after my usual walk in the woods that morning. I did not know who she was, and I reluctantly accepted cookies and milk but refused to go into my now-unfamiliar home. Somehow she got me to my family doctor and later that day to a neurologist, who found my examination normal except for the amnesia and made the diagnosis of TGA, cause unknown. About six hours after its onset and while in the office of the neurologist, the condition abruptly passed and I felt well enough to drive home while my wife related this incredible tale of how I had spent my day. The MRI several days later was normal. Since Lipitor was the only new medicine I was on, the doctor in me made me suspect a possible side effect of this drug and, despite the protestations of the examining doctors that statin drugs did not do this, I stopped the drug. The year passed uneventfully and soon it was time for my next astronaut physical. NASA doctors joined the chorus I had come to expect from physicians and pharmacists during the ensuing year, that statin drugs did not do this, and at their bidding I reluctantly restarted Lipitor at one-half the previous dose. Six weeks later I again descended into the black pit of amnesia, this time for 12 hours and with a retrograde loss of memory back to my high-school days. During that terrible interval, when my entire adult life had been eradicated, I had no awareness of my marriage and four children, my medical school days, my ten adventure-filled years as a USAF flight surgeon, my selection as scientist astronaut or of my post-retirement decade as a writer of medical fiction. The names of my books – like the names of my children – were gone from my mind as completely as if they had never happened. Fortunately and typically for this obscure condition, my memory returned and again I drove home listening to my wife's amazing tale of how my day (and hers) had gone. She said that if I asked her once 'What is happening?' I must have asked her ten thousand times during that terrible period when all recall was lost.

As to recommendations, at the very least, patients on statin drugs and their prescribing doctors must be informed of the potential for impaired brain function. Vigilance on the part of both patient and doctor can only be helpful and may spot a tendency for memory lapses early, but even this can hardly be expected to foresee TGA, which customarily strikes with no warning. It is hardly reassuring that although most of the cognitive case reports occur soon after the statin drug is started or an increase in dosage is made, some of the worst cases have occurred after several trouble-free years on a fixed dosage. One can only caution against the current tendency for ever-increasing use of statin drugs for primary prevention such as we now see in both military and civilian pilots. The mind-robbing potential of this class of drugs is not only theoretical – it is real. Responsible physicians must take heed."

www.spacedoc.net

Nootropics

Nootropics is the name given to a vast array of chemicals that are believed to enhance or preserve brain function in some way. A few of them are prescription drugs that are licensed for particular conditions (for example, vasopressin for bladder control), but most of them are sold as "health supplements" and have not been through the rigorous testing procedure required to qualify them as therapeutic agents. This does not mean they don't work – just that they have not (yet) been researched and developed by major pharmaceutical companies. As far as one can tell (given the lack of formal trials) most of them are fairly safe, but anyone trying them should be aware that they are unproven and might have unwelcome side effects, especially if taken in combination with one another or with other drugs.

Nootropics and their effects

Substance	What it is meant to do	How it is thought to work	Comments
Arginine	Stimulates brain function.	Helps make acetylcholine.	Increases sperm count.
Choline (also Lecithin)	Stimulates brain function.	Helps the brain make acetylcholine.	Do not use if subject to bipolar disorder (manic depression).
Cysteine	Protects brain from "free radical damage" – for example from alcohol and cigarette smoke.	Antioxidant (contains sulphur).	General anti-aging.
Dehydroepian-drosterone (DHEA)	Slows brain degeneration.	"Mother" to wide range of protective hormones.	Anti-tumor and anti-aging.

Ginkgo biloba	Increases blood circulation in the brain.	Delivers more fuel to brain cells.	Some studies suggest it may be helpful for failing memory.
Glutamine	Anti-fatigue.	Acts as emergency "brain food" – glutamic acid is used when glucose is depleted.	High doses may cause gastro-intestinal problems.
Hydergine	Protects brain cells from oxygen damage, increases alertness.	Complex chemical effects increase blood/glucose supply to brain cells.	May cause headache, gastro-intestinal side effects.
Methionine	Protects brain cells.	Antioxidant – contains sulphur.	Some studies suggest antidepressant effect.
Phenylalanine	Reduces anxiety and increases motivation.	Raises dopamine levels.	WARNING: Do NOT use if you are on MAOIs or have a heart condition or high blood pressure.
Piracetam	Enhances general brain function including memory.	One theory is it sensitizes acetylcholine receptors, making more cortical cells more responsive.[18]	One study showed beneficial effect in dyslexic children.
Sulbutiamine	Improves long-term memory.	Aids electrical conduction between neurons. Thought to stimulate hippocampal activity.	May cause wakefulness.
Taurine	Improves working and long-term memory.		May cause dizziness or fainting due to low blood pressure.
Vasopressin	Immediate improvement in working memory.	Has widespread effects on neurotransmitter systems, especially those modulating attention and arousal.	Licensed for use for bladder control. Used as inhalant it can produce runny nose, nasal congestion, bowel cramps and diarrhea.

Hormone replacement therapy (HRT)

Many women complain that they become more forgetful after menopause. This seems entirely plausible because naturally occurring estrogen helps keep brain cells healthy, and at menopause its levels decline drastically. The hormone supplement industry was built partly on the premise that replacement estrogen could keep women's minds sharp.

The evidence for this claim is, however, very confusing indeed. In one study, researchers who tested more than 800 menopausal women (who were not using HRT) over two years found that their memories were fine. In fact, the women's scores improved slightly during the study period.[19] Another study found that women *did* seem to suffer memory loss during menopause, but that taking estrogen did nothing to prevent it.[20] Other studies have found that HRT does prevent memory loss, and that the hormone also preserves cells in the all-important memory center, the hippocampus.

The reason for all the confusion may be that it is not so much memory that takes a dip during menopause but women's capacity to *learn*. The Women's Health Initiative Memory Study, a large longitudinal study funded by the U.S. National Institutes of Health that has been monitoring 10,000 women over the age of 69, suggests that estrogen does enhance the ability to take in new information.

In addition to its possible benefits on memory, taking estrogen during and after menopause reduces the risk of osteoporosis and it may reduce heart disease – although some recent studies have cast doubt on this. On the downside, estrogen can raise the risk of breast cancer. The amount of the increased risk, however, is still unclear. In the end, the decision to take HRT involves balancing the expected benefits against the potential risks.

No hormone   **Testosterone**   **Estrogen**

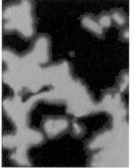

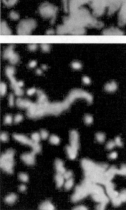
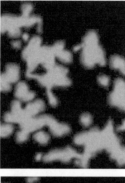
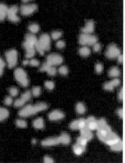

Effects of estrogen and testosterone

The male hormone, testosterone, seems to protect brain cells from dying in much the same way as its female equivalent, estrogen. The top row of images (left) shows three samples of brain cells, tinted gray. The researchers manipulated the cells, sending them on a course to die. Then they administered either no hormones, testosterone or estrogen. The bottom row highlights in white the brain cells that died. Notice that many cells died in the sample that received no hormone, but this cell death was limited in the testosterone and estrogen samples. The research indicates that, like estrogen, testosterone can help preserve brain cells.[21]

Part Four
How to remember

1. Types of memory aids

"She glances at the photo, and the pilot light of memory flickers in her eyes."

Frank Deford, sportswriter

Which aids should I use and when?

Memory aids may be either internal (mental) or external. External aids include making notes, keeping a calendar and even using books and directories. Learning to use external aids is a skill in its own right, and one that is becoming more and more important as our computer-oriented culture demands us to process information rather than store it internally.

Mental disciplines that help you to remember things are called mnemonics. Some mnemonics exploit the web-like nature of human memory by linking new items to those already stored in long-term memory. Others make use of the brain's tendency to organize information into "chunks" and/or narrative form. Some help to "spread" the information throughout the web, for example, by linking words (normally processed only in the left hemisphere) to rhythm and rhyme (processed in the right hemisphere), or by using the brain's strong powers of visualization.

If you use the aids described in this section, provided that your brain is essentially healthy, you will find they greatly enhance your ability to stow away large amounts of information. Remember, though, the prime function of memory as intended by nature is not to create a database. Rather it is to enable you to extract from your experience those things that may be useful in the future, and to make them available so they can guide your actions. In other words, memory is there to make you wiser. Learning information in bulk and being able to retrieve it on cue may be useful for passing exams and for doing some kinds of (usually rather uncreative) work. But if the information is not fully integrated with all the other knowledge that you hold in your head – including knowledge about when, and how, and *why* to use it – it will not "inform" your life. For example, a person might become an extremely competent doctor by learning the facts and skills required to practice medicine, but fail to be a *brilliant* physician because their

Use page 170 of this book to carry out your own simple memory exercises. Make a list of, for example, what you had to eat for the past few meals, jotting down all the ingredients of the dish, what the food tasted like and anything unusual about the dishes. Exercises such as this, when practiced daily, can help form memory "habits"; training the olfactory (smell) and taste pathways for example, helps to build strong memories.

knowledge is not held in a historical and ethical context that would allow them to innovate or to employ it sensitively.

If facts are worth learning, they are worth learning well. That is, they need to be *understood*, in the breadth and depth of one's full contextual knowledge about the world. The information needs to be *examined* as well as ingested; *interpreted*, as well as stored. A headful of facts may be useful in certain specific situations. But if your ambition is to function better in the world, you would do better to concentrate on developing the faculties and habits of mind that form the basis of a good memory.

Keys to a good memory

Use the following practical tips and tricks to help you remember specific things:

Interest, attention and emotional engagement

Your memory, as we have seen, can only be as good as your ability to experience the world. If you are attending to events, the brain will automatically lay them down – or at least their important elements – for future use. The wider your interests and the more actively you engage with them, the denser and bigger the memory "net" you develop will be. Hence new information will be more likely to find a place to lodge in your brain.

Ordering experience

Experience can, in effect, be "doubled up" by thinking about it as it happens. Make a mental note of information or events you want to hold on to as soon as possible after the experience, as though you have a notebook in your head. This will help to focus your attention and organize the information into a form that will make it easier to access later.

Repetition and rehearsal

Every time you recall something you fix it more firmly in your memory. Make a habit of running over events you want to recall, or repeating information, at the end of every day.

Learn little and often

The brain needs time to assimilate new information. So if you have to learn a new skill or digest a lot of data, do it in several short sessions, punctuated by periods of review, rather than by "cramming."

Keep socially, physically and intellectually active

Seek out other people and engage as often as possible in social activities that challenge and stretch your mind. Those that combine physical activity with social engagement are best of all – dancing, rambling, amateur dramatics, for example. Avoid routine, and get into the habit of creating memory "games" from everyday experiences, using examples such as grocery lists, the street names you pass on your drive home, or car license plates. It is also a good idea to challenge your mind by trying to solve a crossword or some other puzzle every day.

Using external aids

Making lists or writing reminder notes to yourself is one of the most widespread of the external memory aids, but list-making is primarily helpful as a way of organizing and laying down information, rather than as an aid to retrieval. More often than not, people do not actually use the list or note to "remember" things – it seems that the act of making it is sufficient to aid later recall.

However, there are situations where list-making appears appropriate but is not in fact the best strategy. For example, one study found that waitresses who went from table to table to take drink orders were much better at remembering the orders if they visualized the drinks in particular locations rather than when they just wrote the orders down.[1]

In general, external aids are regarded as easier to use, more accurate and more dependable than mental strategies. However, with the exception of note-taking, there has been little research into the effectiveness of external memory aids. The most that can be said is that, by and large, people believe they can be effective (with the emphasis, perhaps, on "can").

One problem with external aids is that most of them are highly specific in their use. Their effective operation also requires good habits.

Times to use external memory aids

There are many occasions when trying to hold information "in mind" makes no sense at all. After all, why clog up your brain with information when you can keep it in an external "memory"? Use an external database in the following situations:

- If the information is the sort that *you do not want* to encode long-term, such as a telephone number you know you will use only once.

- When there is a long time between laying down the information and needing to recall it, such as when you make an appointment a long time in advance.

- When you need to keep very precise details, such as if you are acting as the "reporter" of an event, or want later to replicate something you have seen.

- When strict timing is called for, such as when you want to catch the start of a short news bulletin on the radio or television.

- When you need to mull over information to make sense of it, such as digesting a lecture.

- When you don't have time to repeat, rehearse and lay down an item because other events are crowding in.

Types of external aids

The following external aids can be used to help you remember things:

- **Notebooks** are useful for jotting down reminders to yourself – provided you look at them regularly.

- **Alarm clocks and timers** – even watches and cell phones with alarms – can all be helpful in reminding you to do things.

- **Planners, wall calendars and electronic organizers** help you to plan your life and remember the arrangements you have made.

- Some people find **"dry-erase" message boards** placed at key points around the house helpful.

- **Alarm devices** that will make a noise when you clap or whistle can be attached to keys or purses so you can locate them easily.

- **Labels on cupboards and drawers** may help you to remember where you keep things.

- **Pill organizers** are available, some of which include an alarm reminder system, to help you remember to take medication.

- **Keeping a journal** might help you to remember what you have been doing and who you have seen. It may also become a rewarding hobby in its own right.

- Some people find it useful to record ideas or messages onto a **pocket cassette recorder**.

- Carrying a **camera** with you allows you to "snap" moments that might otherwise be forgotten.

2. Mnemonics

"If the face is RED, raise the HEAD.
If the face is PALE, raise the TAIL."

Mnemonic taught to medical students for treatment of fainting

What are mnemonics?

Mnemonics are simply ways of ordering new information to make it easier to recall. We all use them, often automatically. When you dial a familiar telephone number, for example, you probably recall it in chunks: three or four figures at a time, rather than the whole string. And one or more of those chunks might be linked in your mind to a meaningful combination of figures – part of your birthdate, say. When you write the word "conceived" you may recall the mnemonic "i before e except after c." And if you were asked to say how many days there are in the month of June, the chances are you would run through a little rhyme that starts, "Thirty days has September...."

Tricks like this exploit the brain's natural way of processing incoming information. For example, dividing up a telephone number makes it easier to remember because the brain cannot hold more than five to seven things in mind at the same time – three "chunks" of numbers is therefore easier to remember than ten separate digits. Similarly, acronyms such as "UNESCO" are easier to remember than the lengthy "United Nations Educational, Scientific and Cultural Organization." And it is much easier to remember the six-word phrase "i before e except after c" than the spelling of thousands of separate words in which "i" and "e" appear next to one another.

The use of melody, rhythm and rhyme help because they ensure that information is stored in both hemispheres, rather than just the left one that usually deals with words. Hence when the tune or rhythm is recalled, the words "pop out" with it. To demonstrate this, hum a tune you know very well – a Christmas carol or your favorite pop song, say. Can you do it *without* the words running through your head?

Visualization is also very important. If someone refers to "that little store on Main Street next to the movie theater," the obvious way to recall it is to conjure up a picture of that part of town. Those who pay attention to their surroundings and deliberately make visual "notes" of the places they pass will have a far more vivid set of such images to assist them. The same is true of the other senses. Memories are stored in the sensual areas of the brain that first registered the event, so whatever it is, it is more likely to come to mind if those same areas are stimulated. Even dry facts, such as the date of the Battle of Gettysburg, were originally learned in a sensual way – through the voice of a teacher, accompanied, perhaps, by the dusty smell of a classroom. If you can't recall the date although you "know you know" it, spending a few seconds recreating the sound and smell of the classroom may well bring it back. One simple mnemonic trick, if you are cramming for an exam, is to wear a very strong and distinctive perfume while you are learning. Then, during the test, dab a bit of the same scent on your wrist and sniff it when you need a bit of a memory boost (see also pages 166–68).

Creating links

If a new idea is linked to something that is already very familiar, it is much easier to recall. A telephone number that contains a relevant "chunk" – the number of your house, for example – will come to mind much more readily than a string of numbers containing no familiar combination. Systems that employ this type of linkage have a long and glorious history. Before the printing press, huge bodies of knowledge were passed on through the generations by oral teaching alone, and those entrusted with the task of carrying this information learned hugely sophisticated mnemonic systems that allowed them to retain and recall it. They are the same systems employed today by memory champions who can recite whole phone books.

World Memory Championships

Scientist Dr. Eleanor Maguire of University College London looked at the brains of eight people who were leading contenders in the "World Memory Championships" – an event that involves memorizing thousands of random numbers, epic poems and hundreds of unrelated words. The study showed nothing out of the ordinary about the subjects' brains, and they were not in general more intelligent than other people. Their powers were due entirely to their expertise in mnemonics.[2]

Using mnemonics

The human brain is, among other things, a story-making machine. Linking information in sequence, with meaningful links between each part, is the most natural way for it to encode new information. Mnemonic techniques that exploit this include:

Acronyms

These are formed by taking the first letter from several associated words to form a new word. They are particularly useful if you need to remember titles, groups of items or lists of things in a particular order. Some examples of common acronyms include ASPCA (American Society for the Prevention of Cruelty to Animals), REM (rapid eye movement) and LASER (Light Amplification by Stimulated Emission of Radiation).

You can make acronyms out of nearly anything. If you wanted to remember all the mnemonic techniques listed here, for example, you could arrange the first letters of each one to form the word "SARCASM" (**S**entences/**A**crostics, **R**hyming, **C**hunking, **A**cronyms, **S**ongs, **M**ethod of Loci). Perfect acronyms are ones that link to the subject matter, such as RAM (random-access memory in computers); SEAL: Sea, Air and Land teams (U.S. Navy). Let us suppose that you want to memorize the lobes of the brain: frontal, parietal, occipital and temporal. These give you the initial letters FPTO, which do not arrange themselves into anything very useful. However, you can cheat a bit by adding the "a" after the P in "parietal" and then juggle the letters to make the fairly apt: "OF-PaT."

Sentences/acrostics

Like acronyms, you use the first letter of each word you are trying to remember. Instead of making a new word, though, you use the letters to make a sentence. Every Good Boy Does Fine, for example, is a sentence used by novice musicians to remember the notes EGBDF in the order they occur on the treble clef.

Like acronyms, acrostics can be very simple to remember and are particularly helpful when you need to recall a list in a specific order. One advantage over acronyms is that they are less limiting. If your words don't form easy-to-remember acronyms, using acrostics may be preferable. On the other hand, they can take more thought to create and require remembering a whole new sentence rather than just one word (as is the case with acronyms). Otherwise, they present the same problem as acronyms in that they aid memorization but not comprehension. For example (DRAMA):

Does anyone realize all the

Ridiculous things

Actors and actresses

Must endure before hearing the

Applause

Rhymes and songs

Rhythm, repetition, melody and rhyme aid memory because these things are mainly processed in the right hemisphere of the brain, whereas word-based "semantic" information is largely processed in the left hemisphere. Linking the two things therefore effectively "spreads" the information throughout the brain. Using these techniques can be fun, particularly for people who are creative. Rhymes and songs draw on your auditory memory and may be particularly useful for those who can learn tunes, songs or poems easily. Like other techniques they emphasize learning by "rote," not understanding. The following **mnemonic** is used by pilots to remind them that if temperature or pressure drops, their craft will be lower (in altitude) than the aircraft's instruments suggest if they are left uncorrected. On the other hand, a rise in temperature or pressure will result in the opposite effect:

> **High to Low; look out below.**
> **Low to High; clear blue sky.**

This one is a useful little weather tip:

> **Rainbow in the morning: travelers take warning.**
> **Rainbow at night: travelers' delight.**

Rainbows indicate humid air. A morning rainbow is seen in the west – the direction from which storms generally come – and thus often appears before bad weather. Evening rainbows, which appear in the east, usually indicate the passing of stormy weather.

Chunking

This is a technique that is generally used when remembering numbers, although it can be used for remembering other things as well. It is based on the idea that short-term memory is limited as to the number of things that it can hold. A common rule is that a person can remember five to seven things at one time. You may notice that local telephone numbers have seven digits. This is convenient because it is the average amount of numbers that a person can keep in his or her mind at one time.

Australian aborigines and mnemonics

The Australian aborigines traditionally use a mnemonic system to find their way across vast distances mapped only in their memories. Every area has a song associated with it, and each rock and crack along the way is linked to a particular line of the song. The traveler therefore knows their location by their place in the song.

When you use "chunking," you decrease the number of items you are holding in short-term memory by increasing the size of each item. To remember the number string 64831996, you could try thinking about the string as 64 83 19 96 (creating easy to remember "chunks" of numbers). This breaks the group into a smaller number of chunks, so instead of remembering eight individual numbers, you are remembering four larger numbers. This is particularly helpful when you form "chunks" that are meaningful or familiar to you (in this case, the last four numbers in the series are "1996," which can be remembered as one chunk of information).

Method of loci

This technique was used by ancient orators to remember speeches, and it combines the use of organization, visual memory and association. Before using the technique, you must identify a common path that you walk. This can be the route from your home to your work, a walk around your garden, or even the route from your living room to your kitchen. What is essential is that you have a vivid visual memory of both the path and a number of permanent "landmarks" that lie along its route. These may be, for example, a mailbox or a crosswalk; a tree or step; or – if your route is inside – a particular door, shelf or lamp. Once you have determined your path, imagine yourself walking along it, and note the landmarks very carefully in your mind, "fixing them" in place.

Once you have done this you can start to use the path to remember things. This is done by mentally associating each piece of information that you need to remember with one of these landmarks. For example, if you are trying to remember a list of mnemonics, you might remember the first – acronyms – by picturing a laser beam emerging from the mouth of the mailbox to remind you of LASER (an acronym for Light Amplification by Stimulated Emission of Radiation).

Method of loci exercise

1. *Ask someone to read a list of ten words to you at a slow but steady pace (about one word per second). Rather than using any of the memory techniques presented here, simply try to concentrate on the words and remember them. How many words did you remember?*
2. *Now take a few minutes to identify a path or object that you can use in the method of loci. Familiarize yourself with each of the sections of your path or object. Mentally go through each of the locations and visualize them as best you can. Remember, it is important to be able to visualize and recall each location readily. Once you have done this, ask your friend to read you a different list of words. This time, try to create visual images of the words associated with one of the locations. It is likely that, once you become familiar with using this technique, you will be able to remember many more words (maybe all ten items).*

3. Tips and tricks

"Don't agonize. Organize."

Florynce Kennedy, political activist

Practical techniques for remembering names

As we have seen (see page 79), remembering people is a complicated process that can easily go wrong. Difficulty in recalling names is particularly common because information about a person – the elements of recognition – are accessed in a particular order, and names come towards the end. It is also one of the most discomforting memory problems, because when people realize you have forgotten their name they naturally tend to feel belittled or insulted. Conversely, being remembered, and greeted by name, makes a person feel valued and in turn prompts them to value the person who has remembered them.

As with all memories, you can only recall what you have laid down. So if you want to recognize a person, next time you meet them, concentrate on making a firm memory of them, as well as remembering the following tips:

Find out a person's name when you are first introduced

Always make sure you find out the name of a new acquaintance when you are first introduced. If you are not sure that you have caught it correctly, ask for it to be repeated immediately. Repeat it back to make sure you have heard it accurately. If it is an unusual name, ask how it is spelled, and repeat the spelling back. Thereafter repeat the person's name several times during your initial conversation: "Do you live locally, James?" "James, can I get you another drink?" and so on. Bear in mind, though, that some people find it intensely irritating to be repeatedly addressed by name. If you sense this is the case (pick up your cue from surrounding conversations), you can do almost as well by repeating their name *silently*.

Link a new person's name to someone you know

Remembering a new name is easier to do if you link it to that of a mutual acquaintance. For example, if you know Jane and she introduces you to Zoe, make a visual note of the two of them together. Establish their relationship with other people you know ("Do you know many people here?" is a very useful icebreaker in this regard) and spend a little time "slotting in" the new person to your existing circle of acquaintances.

Link a person's name to a physical feature or characteristic

If a person has a resemblance to something – fishy eyes, elfin ears, features, a moon-shaped face – find some way to link their name to that feature. If there is no obvious connection, stretch your imagination to contrive one. For example, if the person's name is Cookson and they are very thin, imagine them as the son of a cook who forgot to cook for his children. The stranger the idea the more memorable it will be.

Celebrity connections

If you are introduced to someone who shares a name with someone famous, imagine this new person in the place of the celebrity … again, the more absurd the image this presents, the better. If you meet a man named "Monroe," for example, take a second to imagine him dressed in a fifties' style dress that is being blown up by air from a vent. Remember – the person before you need never know what is in your mind, so you can make your links as crazy as you like.

Ask again

If you run into someone whose name you have forgotten, ask them again what they are called. It isn't bad to ask them again, but try some of the memory clues to see if you can remember it for the next time you run into them!

Quick guide to remembering names

1. Repeat the person's name during your conversation with them and several times in your head.
2. Associate their name with the person they are with.
3. Link their name to a characteristic or something they look like.
4. Associate their name with the name of someone famous.
5. Ask for their name again when you see them.

Mnemonics really work

for remembering the Great Lakes:

HOMES

(**H**uron, **O**ntario, **M**ichigan, **E**rie, **S**uperior)

for the date of Columbus' voyage:

In 1492, Columbus sailed the ocean blue.

for the colors of the rainbow:

Roy G. Biv

(**R**ed, **o**range, **y**ellow, **g**reen, **b**lue, **i**ndigo, **v**iolet)

Feed your brain

While so-called memory superfoods and natural remedies for more effective memory have been ruled out by many medical practitioners, there is generally some understanding that a good diet rich in antioxidants is one way to improve the chances of having a better memory. By looking after yourself in general it is possible to avoid certain diseases and conditions associated with a poor memory (see pages 120–24 for some examples of memory-debilitating diseases).

It is perhaps more useful to combine diet with exercise and plenty of sleep (see page 127 for an explanation of how good sleep improves memory). Not only does fatigue interfere with memory, but it may also make it harder to recall information stored in our long-term memory, including things we know well.

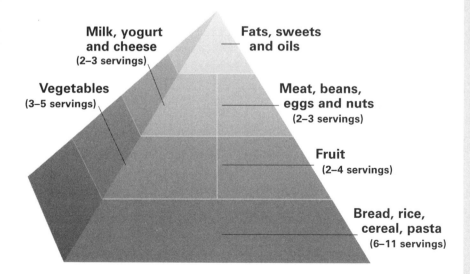

Milk, yogurt and cheese
(2–3 servings)

Fats, sweets and oils

Vegetables
(3–5 servings)

Meat, beans, eggs and nuts
(2–3 servings)

Fruit
(2–4 servings)

Bread, rice, cereal, pasta
(6–11 servings)

There is plenty of evidence that adequate amounts of protein, carbohydrates and vitamins (vitamin B1 in particular) are essential for many chemical processes that occur in the brain in lay-down, recall and remembering things. It is therefore important to have a well-balanced diet combining all the major food groups.

Notes

Quick memory test score (pages 114–15)

1 *Give yourself 1 point for remembering the exact date.*

2/16 *Give yourself 1 point for each correct answer (orange, television, cushion), total 3 points.*

3 *If the difference between your guessed time and the correct time is less than 30 minutes, give yourself 1 point. If it is over 30 minutes, score zero.*

4 *Award 1 point for each president named correctly (total 5 points): George W. Bush, Bill Clinton, George H. W. Bush, Ronald Reagan, Jimmy Carter. The order is not important.*

5 *Award 1 point for each correct answer (total 8 points):
top row (l to r) 1) acorn, 2) compass, 3) whistle, 4) igloo;
bottom row (l to r) 5) scales, 6) spatula, 7) planet, 8) easel.*

6 *Give yourself 1 point for remembering your last address.*

7 *Give yourself 1 point if you answered "yes."*

8–15 *Give yourself 1 point for every "no" answer (total 8 points).*

Result
27 or 28: *Your memory (as far as this test measures it) is fine.*

22–26: *You may have some memory difficulties. If they persist and are causing inconvenience or making you inefficient or embarrassed, it is a good idea to ask your doctor to arrange for you to have a full evaluation.*

21 or less: *Your result suggests some memory impairment. Please seek a full evaluation.*

Notes to the Text

Part One

[1] Geiselman, R., Fisher, R., "Ten years of cognitive interviewing," *Intersections in Basic and Applied Memory Research*, Payne, D., Conrad, F. (eds), Lawrence Erlbaum, 1996.

Part Two

[1] *Psychology and Aging*, December 2002, American Psychological Association.

[2] Cabeza, R., Anderson, N.D., Locantore, J.K., McIntosh, A.R., "Aging gracefully: compensatory brain activity in high-performing older adults," *Neuroimage,* November 2002, 17, 3, 1394–402.

[3] Cabeza, R., Kapur, S., Craik, F.I.M., McIntosh, A.R., Houle, S., Tulving, E., "Functional neuroanatomy of recall and recognition: A PET study of episodic memory," *Journal of Neuroscience*, 1997, 9, 254–265.

[4] Schutte, A.R., Spencer, J.P., Schoner, G., "Testing the dynamic field theory: working memory for locations becomes more spatially precise over development," summarized from *Child Development*, 2003, 74: 5, The Society for Research in Child Development.

[5] Anderson, M.C., et al., "Neural systems underlying the suppression of unwanted memories," *Science*, January 9, 2004, 303: 20, 232–235.

[6] Ochberg, F.M., Department of Psychiatry, Michigan State University, "The counting method for ameliorating traumatic memories," *Journal of Trauma Stress*, October 1996, 4: 873–880.

[7] Research presented at Society for Neuroscience Meeting, New Orleans, September 2003.

Part Three

[1] Barker, A., Jones, R., Jennison, C., "A prevalence study of age-associated memory impairment," *British Journal of Psychiatry*, 1995, 167, 642–648.

[2] Gary Small, M.D., director, UCLA Center on Aging.

[3] Haan, M.N., Shemanski, L., Jagust, W.J., Manolio, T.A., "The role of APOE 4 in modulating effects of other risk factors for cognitive decline in elderly persons," JAMA 1999, 282: 40–46.

[4] Butler, R., et al., *Neuron*, September 30, 2004.

[5] Bickel, H., "The heirarchic dementia scale," *International Psychogeriatrics* 8, 213–224.

[6] Engelgau, M.N., Narayan, V., Gregg, E.W., "Complications of diabetes in elderly people," *British Medical Journal*, October 26, 2002, 325: 7370, 916–917.

[7] Study carried out jointly by Christopher Ryan, professor of psychiatry at the University of Pittsburgh School of Medicine, and Dr. Mark Strachan of Western General Hospital, Edinburgh. Presented at the American Diabetes Association's annual meeting, Florida, June 2003.

[8] Gould, E., Wooley, C.S., McEwen, B.S., "The hippocampal formation: morphological changes induced by thyroid, gonadal and adrenal hormones," *Psychoneuroendocrinology*, 1991, 16: 1–3, 67–84.

[9] Boillet, D., Szoke, A., "Psychiatric manifestations as the only clinical sign of hypothyroidism. Apropos of case." (French) *Encephale*, 1998, 24: 1, 65–8.

[10] Cho, K., "Chronic 'jet lag' produces temporal lobe atrophy and spatial cognitive deficits," *Nature Neuroscience*, June 2001, 4: 6, 567–568.

[11] Erkinjuntti, T., et al., "Efficacy of galantamine in probable vascular dementia and Alzheimer's disease combined with cerebrovascular disease: a randomized trial," *Lancet*, April 13, 2002, 359: 9314, 1283–1290.

[12] Eriksson, P.S., Perfilieva, E., Bjork-Eriksson, T., Alborn, A.M., Nordborg, C., Peterson, D.A., Gage, F.H., "Neurogenesis in the adult human hippocampus," *Nature Medicine*, November 1998, 4,1313–7.

[13] Podewils, L.J., Lyketsos, C.G., Department of Epidemiology and Mental Hygiene, The Johns Hopkins School of Medicine, "Tricyclic antidepressants and cognitive decline," *Psychosomatics 2002,* January to February, 43:1, 31–35.

[14] Wolozin, B., Kellman, W., Rousseau, P., Celesia, G.G., Siegel, G., "Decreased prevalence of Alzheimer's disease associated with 3-Hydroxy-3-Methyglutaryl Coenzyme A reduced inhibitors," *Archives of Neurology*, 2000, 57, 1439–1443.

[15] Zornberg, G.L., Seshadri, Jick, S.S., Seshadri, S., Drachman, D.A., *Lancet* 2000, 356, 1627–31.

[16] Wagstaff, L.R., Mitton, M. W., McLendon, B., Murali, P. Doraiswamy, "Statin-Associated Memory Loss: Analysis of 60 Case Reports and Review of the Literature," *Pharmapsycotherapy*, July 23, 2003, 7, 871–80.

[17] ref 16.

[18] Dilanni, M. et al., "The effects of Piracetam in Children with Dyslexia," *Journal of Clinical Psychopharmacology*, 1985, 5, 272–8.

[19] Meyer, P.M., Powell, L.H., Wilson, R.S., Everton-Rose, S.A., Kravitz, H.M., Luborsky, J.L., Madden, T., Pandey, D., Evans, D.A., "A population-based longitudinal study of cognitive functioning in the menopausal transition," *Neurology*, 2003, 61, 801–806.

[20] Shumaker, S.A., et al., "Estrogen plus progestin and the incidence of dementia and mild cognitive impairment in postmenopausal women. The women's health initiative memory study: a randomized controlled trial," *Journal of the American Medical Association*, 2003, 289, 2651–2662.

[21] Hammond, J., Goodyer, C., Le, Q., Gelfand, M., Trifiro, M., LeBlanc, A., "Testosterone-mediated neuroprotection through the androgen receptor in human primary neurons," *Journal Neurochemistry*, 2001, 77, 1–9.

Part Four

[1] Intons-Peterson, M.J., Fourrier, J., "External and internal memory aids: when and how often do we use them?," *Journal of Experimental Psychology*, 115, 267–280.

[2] Maguire, E., et al., "Routes to remembering," *Nature Neuroscience* January 2003, 6, 90–95.

Picture credits

Page 35: Claude Nuridsany and Marie Perennou/Science Photo Library

Page 40 (bottom): Christian Darkin/Science Photo Library

Page 40 (top): Christian Darkin/Science Photo Library

Page 116: Alfred Pasieka/Science Photo Library

Page 145: Jennifer Hammond, Quynh Le, Cindy Goodyer, Morie Gelfand, Mark Trifiro, Andrea LeBlanc, "Testosterone-mediated neuroprotection through the androgen receptor in human primary neurons," *Journal Neurochemistry*, 2001, 77, 1–9.

Publisher's acknowledgments

The publisher gratefully acknowledges the permission granted to reproduce the copyright material in this book. Every effort has been made to trace the copyright holders and to obtain permission for the use of copyright material. The publisher apologizes for any errors or omissions and would be grateful if notified of any corrections that should be incorporated in future reprints or editions of the book.

Index